If You Love To Live, Then Learn To Love

By

A.C. Johnson MD

If You Love To Live,

Then Learn To Love

By

A.C. Johnson MD

 All Scriptures are taken from the New International Version, New Living Translation, and King James Version of the Bible, unless otherwise specified.

Author A.C. Johnson can be reached via email at *johnops51@yahoo.com*

He cordially invites you to visit his web sites

1] www.healingfacts.org

2] www.healingfacts.com

3] www.healingfacts.net

If You Love To Live,

Then Learn To Love

By

A.C. Johnson MD

Assisted by

Bessie S Johnson

S.C. Johnson

Albert Johnson

Vasantha Chella

Nesadoss Johnson

Samuel Johnson

Albert Johnson

Beulah Johnson

Augustine Johnson

Rajkumar Johnson

Ebenezer Johnson

Andrew Johnson

Elizabeth George

Joanna George

Joshua 24:15 (TLB)

15 But if you are unwilling to obey the Lord, then **decide today whom you will obey**.

Will it be the gods of your ancestors beyond the Euphrates or the gods of the Amorites here in this land?

But as for me and my family, we will serve the Lord."

CONTENTS

Introduction

It will aid our understanding if we are made aware of the fact that there are two major kinds of love. The Greek language however classified 'love' into three parts [1] *Agape* love meaning godly love [2] Filial love, meaning love between the family members and [3] Erotic love, meaning love between sexual partners. But in the present day language and communication, there are numerous ways in which 'love' is implied, diluting the most meaningful of words into a most insipid one.

1. The origin of love is **Celestial.**

   Therefore, the original love is Celestial.

   The King James Version of the Bible calls this love as **Charity**

   The word charity is hardly used these days; substituted by the word 'love', it is often misunderstood and misused.

2. The counterfeit love is **Terrestrial love**.

   This love is subdivided into expressing many deep and superficial emotions.

Chapter 1

Terrestrial love :

Love is the word used by all to express not only our emotions, but also our desires. The word is used by psychotic killers and rapists, self centered people and the saintly. It is a word used from a small child to the old. It is also the word used by men, women and children of all ages to express their good sentiments in addressing their partners and parents. It is also a word used loosely to express one's woozy feelings for good food, alcohol, or drugs. It is also used to express animal appetites, or to refer to animal pets, and even inanimate objects like cars, boats, dress, boots and make up kits.

The Greeks as mentioned earlier, used different words to differentiate different types of love- *agape* love meaning love for God, filial love for the family, erotic love for sexual attraction. These terms however did not become established in popular usage. The popular practise has been to interchange the hollow and shallow word such as 'like' with the profound word 'love'. So much so, we hear sentences like "I love movies", "I love burgers" or "I love to have my back scratched!" The usage here is not only frivolous but is degrading to the profound emotional meaning of the word 'love'.

We are all born with self love, which enables self preservation in order to protect and nourish us to growth toward maturity. A new born baby wants to be fed, held, loved, and cleaned. Till nearly 2 to 3 years it is natural for the child to be centered only on self and security for self. Smiles and cuddles are given in exchange to the adults who care for the baby, in order to get attention for self. A realization dawns in the child that when the child shows love or affection, it is returned to it, multiplied many times. Parents and care givers imprint this message upon the child's mind. This is the time the parents should train the infant to share things with others, especially siblings, and not to be selfish.

A wrong message can be handed down to the child by parents who are dysfunctional, or by those showing partiality to the children, arising from their own selfishness and retarded 'mentation'. As children grow older and learn to play games, they should be taught to learn the rules and obey them. They also need to be taught not to be solo players, but team players, who can pass the ball to another to make a touch down or shoot a goal. Gradual maturation is given to the children growing into the teens and adult life on to old age. Failure of proper education will only bring out the monsters within us, to ruin us and our society.

The next stage of our maturity comes when falling in love with a future life partner. This time attention from 'self' has an opportunity of being transferred to another, other than self. This transference is made easier by the pleasurable gift of sex between the legitimate partners, meaning husband and wife. Once the initial excitement of sex is over, the special grand passion between them cools down, and the caliber and grade of love change. But if the marriage and commitment have a deeper level of love than mere passion, with God's approval and blessing, the emotion between the partners stays. Tenderness and deep bonding of friendship develop and hold the couple together even as they grow older, wrinkled in looks and crippled in body and also weak in sexual ability.

There are still more ways that lead us to understand what love really is, from a terrestrial to a celestial point of view.

As children are born to parents through parents' sexual act and pleasure, they tend to steal a significant amount of time the parents could have had for themselves. The infants put a heavy toll on the time and energy of the parents in their growing process. This is really the time during which the parents are given the opportunity to mature in a non sexual love relation with the fruits of their past sexual love. This parental love becomes one of 'giving one's self sacrificially'. Parents will risk their lives even for children who are unable or unwilling to return the parental love for them. This takes the parents closer to learning the celestial meaning of love. Yet sadly there are parents, even mothers, who kill their children because the children come in their way of enjoying their freedom and pleasure. This behavior is also called "love" by the abusers.

God so loves us, that He wants us humans to share His love. God's ways are far different from ours. So, we need to be taught like babies to grow into the fullness of heavenly living. We are being taken through the world and its understanding of love into heaven's standard of love. Passion is the intensity of the emotion, and is often mistaken to be the same as love. Passion is the driving force, a deep desire that motivates us. Compassion indicates the real depth of emotion, when selfishness is got rid of.

The following are the words used to represent love:

Affection
Like
Fond of
Longing
Desiring
Wanting
Craving
Crush
Infatuation
Attraction
Mate seeking

Soul-mate
Admiration

Yet, love is something different:

- Sex is not love.
- Copulation is not love.
- Infatuation is not love.
- Covetousness is not love
- Wanting is not love.
- Desire is not love.
- Attachments are not love.
- Giving, in order to receive is not love – but a business and a bargain.

Greed for 'a thing' owned by another is covetousness. Greed and envy for what `a person' is, is jealousy.

Many people loosely use the words sex and love as denoting the same. Are love and sex the same? We need to examine these two entities. Some dictionaries put all the above-described emotions as synonyms for love, an unfortunate tendency.

Chapter 2

Sex is a gift from God to His creation.

What is sex?

Sex is a physical act performed by individuals to bring pleasure to one's own self. God created male and female, so that there would not only be meaningless self-pleasure and 'recreation', but a greater purpose called "Re-creation" of the species. To humans, God gave the pleasure of sex to make them start sharing with God, in His plan of creation in an enjoyable and purposeful way. But the devil wanted to mess this good thing called sex, which was given with boundaries, to become a perversion of sex, without boundaries. All perversions and boundary breaking will bring calamities. This is applicable to the entire universe. The act of sex will produce closeness of physical bodies, which is mistaken for intimacy. Having sex is commonly but wrongly referred to as "making love". Love is not something one can 'make' or just 'feel' as and when desired. Love is a choice of life style to be lived, regardless of the cost or consequences.

When does sex operate?

As maturity sets in from childhood to teens, we the earthlings grow into young adults and find a sudden spurt in our growth. Our limbs grow longer, often making us bump into things. Hair starts growing on the face of males. Hair also grows in the axilla and around the genitalia of both males and females. Secondary 'sex organs' undergo maturity both outside and inside our bodies. Breasts start enlarging in females. The secretion of the endocrine takes on a new magnitude and causes surges of emotions, which rack and shake every living creature. Most of the creatures are governed by the sex urge called **lust**. But this is *not* love, though the word **love** is wrongly used. Male elephants develop 'musk' and become rogues in rampage because of this hormonal sex drive. This development is seen in other animals and humans too.

Lust is a desire and an urge that comes in, to 'procreate'. Selection of mate by itself does not constitute love, but is a "passion" evoked, in other words, an attraction, focused on a particular person. Passion is a fluctuating emotion of desire. The degree of passion can vary even to the extent of risking life and reputation, besides sadly over-riding reasoning.

Perverted sex can cause an insane 'urge' to 'merge' with any one or anything to discharge their gonadal secretions and excretion. Such a perverted person would "like" to have sex with any number of sex partners, or partners of the same sex, or with young children, or with animals, or even dead bodies. These perversions have been well documented in medical jurisprudence.

What is sex's destination?

Self centered attitude to be changed

For any person, if the focus is only upon the action, it can become insatiable and unsatisfying, and will take the person into endless perversions. This kind of emotion at best is called as "like to", or as "wanting to". Like as in drug addiction, it causes a perverted 'craving' with no satisfaction.

Growing out of the self centeredness

Another person would "like" to have sex with only one person, namely his or her mate. To have, or, even to consider doing the same with any one else would be revolting to such a person. An element of the emotion called "love" has now entered into their action of sex, taking their relationship into an entirely new dimension.

Wanting something very badly or, liking something desperately, is not love. Those feelings of wanting, or, liking, or needing, are due to one's appetite and desire. Love is different from these feelings. We will deal with this as we proceed.

Why is sex given?

Sex is a powerful emotional drive. It is built into our physiology and our psyche. It is given to us human beings to fulfill three purposes by God.

1. To populate the earth with our progenies.

2. To make you and me and our progeny as responsible stewards of the planet earth, into which God has placed us all.

3. God want us humans to learn about celestial love which is totally selfless, holy and geared to spiritual intimacy. Sex is given as a terrestrial love vehicle-complex to help us get over, and out of our self-centered immature nature. We can compare it to the titbits given to dogs and other animals while disciplining and training them to help and collaborate with us, the trainers.

How does sin enter into sex?

A good sex act aims to please and satisfy the need of the other partner. Pleasing only one's self is wrong. For, self-centeredness is a wide-open portal for sin to enter in. Satan, in his effort to alienate us from the holy God, to destroy us, and to damn us for eternity, provides a mirage against God given love, twisting love to lust. To reiterate, sex is then shabbily limited to a physical, bodily sensation triggered on through sight, smell, touch, sound or drugs. The satiation of these sensory demands may result in a temporary relief obtained through gonadal secretions, and excretions of the body, a short existing part of humanity. Sex in such a situation becomes devoid of the more important component of the human being, namely the intimacy between the soul and the spirit, which are the longer living components of human beings.

Chapter 3

The anatomy and the physiology of sexual and spiritual maturity.

There are two sexes, male and female. The male is born with penis, prostate and testes to produce sperms when physical maturity sets in. With maturity, the pituitary gland triggers the testes to secrete androgens and testosterone. This causes facial hair, as beard and mustache growth, and deepening of the voice. Sex urges come into play, with strong attraction toward the female. The female is born with two ovaries, uterus and vagina. When maturity sets in for females, both breasts enlarge, and the ovulation cycle with menstruation starts. Estrogen and progesterone are secreted. The pituitary gland interacts with the other endocrine glands in the body of both male and the female to bring about overall maturity. They also bring the autonomic nervous system link up with sexual activation.

Sex was given to humanity to understand a little about the "ultimate purpose"—which brings along with it the following sequences.

1. This instigates seeking for a mate [spouse],

2. There is waiting, with eager "expectancy" to get the right one,

3. The next is finding a mate, and examining the suitability: "appreciation",

4. The next stage is to establish the right to become the sole mate through commitment.

5. First love, which makes one blind to self and other people except the mate.

6. Learning to understand one another in the body and mind [physically and emotionally].

7. Learning to communicate agreeably with each other despite differences.

All honeymoons are short lived. Physical satiation will follow emotional satiation, for the process of sex [love-making] of the flesh is very brief and limited. This is because the flesh is a weak and temporary vessel. It cannot handle more than its capacity. Therefore the flesh can handle the process of sexual ecstasy which involves rapid heart rate, high blood pressure and churning of the nervous system violently, only for a brief duration. As seen before, sex pleasure gives 'happi'ness as long as it 'happens', and is not sustained or permanent as joy is. In fact till the next hormonal replenishment takes place, sex may be unwelcome.

But, joy and peace are the by products of our celestial love. This celestial love has a spiritual dimension toward our Creator, one that is meant to be shared with other human beings. This 'joy' has an eternal element and quality. It brings a deep spiritual intimacy where sex has no place at all. It is possible to get a glimpse of this joy even on earth. For God has promised to give us peace that surpasses all human understanding and joy which the world cannot give nor take away from us.

In the spiritual realm in heaven, which should be our eternal home, there will be no restriction or limitation of joy, because the limiting flesh will cease to exist. The praise and worship, and the ecstasy of the loving, holy-intimacy, not only between God and mankind, but also between mankind and mankind will become endless and eternal.

Chapter 4

Celestial Love:

What is this real love, also called celestial love?

The Bible says that God is love and that He loves us. So He gave us His Son as His **love** gift. This information has been given to the humanity through the over 2500 year old, Old Testament prophesies in the Bible so that, we can be assured that God keeps His promises through generations.

This makes Celestial love a Celestial gift

Instead of thrusting His great gift called "Love", down our throat as the royal commands by kings, commander or ruler do, God sent His love packed into a little baby born to poor parents in an animal manger. What better way to show us that God leaves the "choice" of accepting, or rejecting this Love, to us?

This makes Celestial love a choice

The noble and sacred word 'love' became so upsetting to Satan that he started messing it up and creating a counterfeit of love, and came up with **lust**. This is what he offered to Eve. We do have a choice to reject lust, but once we delay the rejection, lust takes over to bring us under subjection and subordination.

Watch out for these two counterfeits:

God gave instructions that we should **love God**.

Satan took the first letter "l" from lust and inserted it into the word 'God' before it ended.

Since then, humanity has lusted [perverted love] after go"l"d, ignoring to love our Creator 'God'.

It will be possible to have Celestial love in us only if we receive the Celestial gift called Jesus into our hearts.

To protect us, and to feed us, to grow into maturity, God gave us the **Word** to love.

Satan took the letter "l", perverted it and inserted it into the Word God gave us to love, and perverted us to **love** [lust] the **wor"l"d** and to ignore the Word.

Jesus has confirmed to us that, He is the Word.

Love was and is a word reverently used by saints in relation to God. They acknowledge Love as a uniquely godly emotion, and an action extended from heaven toward us.

Chapter 5

What is the purpose of real love?

Love is not just an emotion, but an eternal mighty force, for it comes from God Himself into the world. This love has two components, and they are joy and peace. Unlike pleasure, which is experienced only as long as the pleasure inducing sensation exists, the love from God brings joy and peace, which will last whether there is an associated physical or mental pleasure or not. The blend of love, joy and peace will merge into forming another heavenly quality called "intimacy".

- Love is the communication channel used by saints to contact God.
- Love is the 'Atmosphere' of heaven, holy and pure.
- Love is the 'Breath' we need to breathe in to live, and breathe out in gratitude to God.
- Love is an unselfish Supreme, giving expression of oneself to another as God Himself did.
- Love is spontaneous self-sacrifice, not expecting any return.
- Love is a Godly emotion, which does not fluctuate.

- Love is God's gift to us, and can be our gift to God.
- Love is the essence of our Worship
- Love is the Lord Jesus who died in our place, taking our sins away from us.

Where does love originate?

Love originates from heaven, from the Father and the Creator God.

The heaven could not contain God's love and it overflowed upon us on earth. This Love had to be in the human form for humanity to recognize and to emulate.

This human incarnation of the Divine love was the Lord Jesus Christ.

He offers to enter into every heart that is willing to receive Him. He brings the power of the Holy Spirit with Him into the hearts to start the Love— the love of heaven into our human hearts.

Love can only flow from within to others outside; for like a mighty fountain, it flows down and not up toward itself. It is directed towards others, and not toward its own "self". Love will not love 'itself', contrary to modern psychological theories. It is easier for water to flow uphill than for real love to love itself.

What is love's destination?

Love's intention is to bring the atmosphere of Heaven into the Earth, so that humanity can have a foretaste of Heaven. John 3: 15-16.

God's love is a sharing, giving love [Charity]

God's infinite gift of love cannot be measured nor understood, neither by terrestrial standards [by us humans], nor by celestial standards [even by angels]. His eventual plans and purposes can be understood only as we get to know God better, as we learn to walk with Him and talk with Him. God really loves us, and would like us to grow into emotional and spiritual maturity. God's gift of love, called inadequately as *agape* love or 'Charity' is intended to bring between two different and distinct human individuals—namely the two different sexes on earth —a physical bonding, an emotional bonding, and then a spiritual fellowship and intimacy. In a human setting at home, the husband and wife are given the unique opportunity to gradually learn to get to know one another, not only physically, but also mentally and spiritually. This process can fuse the two emotionally, even though they will still remain as distinct physical individuals.

The World of Demons

Jesus has warned us that if we drive one demon from within us and not fill our soul with God, that one driven devil will bring seven more deadly demons to take possession of us. Non-Christian Psychologists have conceded that within a single person multiple "personalities" or entities may live. Books have been written on these psychological enigmas. The spirit beings are not confined to a material physical body or bodies. They can move in and out of human matter, which are porous to them.

God is a Spirit Being. He created various levels and grades of spirit beings called angels. The atmosphere of heaven is one of love and holiness. But some of the angels became sinful and left heaven as they could not bear the holiness. These fallen angels are called demons, or evil spirits. Satan is their leader.

God created humans with material human bodies having eternal souls, which are given the freedom of choice to invite and host God's spirit or any evil spirit. We are also given a number of emotions to enrich our lives.

Maturing Love

As mentioned earlier, God has given '**Love**' to us, to be enjoyed on earth and heaven. He packed the heavenly love for us as a tiny baby delivered in a lowly manger two thousand years ago. It was this baby Jesus who taught us how to love, whom to love, and what love really is. Love is the language and atmosphere of heaven and is very much like the 'air' of heaven. Jesus brought heaven to us on earth, mixed it with His holy living. He makes it possible for us to enjoy heaven on earth, when we receive

Him into our hearts. On earth without air, our vocal cords cannot function to communicate, nor can we survive without breathing the air into our lungs. Love and holiness are that important for life in heaven.

We cannot survive in the holy, love atmosphere of heaven with our sinful nature; therefore Jesus came down to pay the penalty for our sins, to pardon and save us and to make us acceptable to live in heaven eternally. We can even have a fore taste of heaven while still on earth. Like Jesus, many martyrs died, forgiving their tormentors and murderers, because they received the love of God into their hearts through Jesus.

Love is not only for recreation, but re-creation, [carrying responsibility].

God has also shown us the power generated by 'love'. The act of even the level of human "sex-love" can bring within it a "re-creation" of God's creation—an offspring. The purpose of this is to take us to the next level of **love**, to make us understand that sex is not the only necessary 'incentive' to make us "love" someone especially those who should not or must not offer sex in return. Satan in his efforts to divert us away from the truth has misrepresented the word LOVE as something of a 'recreation', a world of difference from what God wants it to be: RE-CREATION of God's love.

Chapter 6

Perversion of love:

The devil cannot create any thing good or holy. But he is good at mimicking, imitating and messing up things. He is the force behind those who change the labels such as 'dangerous poison' and puts the label of 'food and grocery' on them. He has done the same thing to the sacred word called 'love'. He is at the back of those who misinterpret and misrepresent the loving word of God. With the result, most criminal activity was given misinterpreted Biblical support, in direct contradiction to the teachings and life of Jesus. The name Christians were given to those who followed the Lord Jesus and took up their crosses to follow Him. The atrocities done under the name of Christianity in the past, the present and the future have nothing to do with God and Jesus Christ. The devils use the word Christianity to mock us and make us do the demonic things, to defy the loving God and to keep us from enjoying eternity in heaven. Having lost their ability to live in heaven, the demons do not want any one else to have the privilege of being in heaven.

Satan holds a mirror in front of us to mis-read God's message of **"Love",** in reverse. With some addition, this easily becomes 'EVOL-'U'-TION'. The underlying theory of evolution implies that God does not exist, So God could not have created us, and therefore, we the humans are not to be held accountable to live a clean and good life. Remember the devil plays his proven game of 'printer's devilishness' over and over again. When man wanted to know – who made him and who cares for him and who is mankind's best friend, God wrote out 'GOD'. Satan again put the mirror before mankind making them read it out in reverse as `dog'. So, the befuddled mankind [fortunately not all] thinks that `dog' should be their best friend. Then the evolutionists fantasy that dogs, animals, birds, insects, reptiles, parasites, bacteria, viruses were precursors to human evolution. The animal food section in super stores and 'protect the animals activists' are increasing rapidly, but not as rapidly as abortion clinics [where humans are killed in millions and the wombs are turned to temporary tombs]. At the same time, MacDonald, KFC, and other fast food chains are increasing. Oxymoronic humanity!

Satan brings an alternative to the Scripture, every few years to make it appealing to the successive generations. For the current generation, psychology has been offered as the alternative. Diseases have been ascribed to an abstract entity [not an organic one like the brain]; organic medications are prescribed for organic bodily diseases. The mind-altering medications have dangerous side reactions, and as only symptomatic and not curative, gets people addicted to drugs. As psychiatry and psychology try to strengthen the 'self' [ego] of the affected person, it works against the scripture, and fails to help. According to this 'science' sin is only an alternative life style with modern evolution of culture.

The definition of LUST is (Love) Lost. Evil cannot exist without our freedom to choose. Love cannot exist in us without our freedom to choose it. Love is a voluntary slave, but enjoys complete freedom. Love does not choose to please, or pamper its own 'self'.

Love for 'self' cannot be called love. It has no freedom for it is in total bondage. It is a slave to 'self', the physical and emotional sensations.

'Free love' is a misnomer till it becomes "Freed Love" that has been able to delete the 'd', accepting death to self. The 'd' stands for devil's entrapment, bringing decay and death.

Law makes one to become an outlaw. For it tells us what are forbidden. Our nature is such that we have a fatal fascination and curiosity to indulge in the forbidden things.

Rom. 7:7-11: "Well then, am I suggesting that the law of God is evil? Of course not! The law is not sinful, but it was the law that showed me my sin. I would never have known that coveting is wrong if the law had not said, "Do not covet." [8] But sin took advantage of this law and aroused all kinds of forbidden desires within me! If there were no law, sin would not have that power.

[9] I felt fine when I did not understand what the law demanded. But when I learned the truth, I realized I had broken the law and was a sinner, doomed to die. [10] So the good law, which was supposed to show me the way of life, instead gave me the death penalty. [11] Sin took advantage of the law and fooled me; it took the good law and used it to make me guilty of death."

Love enables us to get free from this deadly urge to break rules and boundaries and to carryout and fulfill the law, which cannot be fulfilled by any other means.

Rom. 13:10: "Love does no wrong to anyone, so love satisfies all of God's requirements".

1. God loves us unconditionally, regardless of

Where we are
What we are
Who we are

Therefore we can always rejoice over this constant fact.

2. God's love gives us freedom

We need not try to live to placate God.

We are not in bondage to be performing in order to be acceptable to Him.

3. God's love gives us assurance

We are always under the canopy of His love no matter what the circumstances are. This information gives us freedom and power to walk with God in love for Him. For, He accepts us just as we are, if we are willing to receive Him. After that we will never ever be the same. For there are no unlovable saved sinners in God's point of view. In contrast, our point of view is quite different. We well remember the faults of our sinful neighbor! God does not.

Love has no place, or time for 'self' but for the one who is loved – to do the best for the loved one without expecting anything in return; not even thanks.

"Self love" on the contrary is constantly griping that self has been deprived, deceived, despised, downtrodden, damaged (mentally, verbally or physically) and so on.

Affection and deep passions are not real love. For these require reciprocity.

Love makes you loyal regardless of cost to your self
There is no double mindedness in love
Love makes you trust – regardless of situations
Love does not attribute evil to the one who is loved

Love does not register any wrong done to it
Love does not mistrust or carry suspicion of the
one loved
Love makes you not give up but stand up for the
one loved

The good news of the Gospel is the Cross.

For the Cross is the symbol of God's love in supreme Self-sacrifice.

❖ The vertical component is God's love, for humans.

❖ The horizontal component is human, the symbol of all things negative.

When we accept God's love to come into our lives, we come to the Cross of the Lord Jesus who has the power to cross-out our sin and to put God's love into our lives.

† If one's knowledge, faith and surrender do not come to end in the Cross, it does not form the Gospel, which is nothing but divine LOVE.

Chapter 7

Conversion to God's love

LOVE IS LIKE THE FIRE

For GOD IS LOVE'S SIRE

Wood, coal, paper, and gasoline by themselves are not fire. But they can be made to burn. The fire goes out when the gas runs out or when wood turns to ashes. Sun is a fireball and has not gone out for centuries, because of God's love for His creation. For without the sun, our lives will be extinguished.

There is only one God. This one God is present in three distinct persons. To the human mind, which is confined to one physical body, this sounds impossible. But God is a Spirit. We not only need to worship Him in Spirit, but also be willing to understand the infinitely different spirit realm of God who is not only omnipotent and omniscient, but also omnipresent.

How does one God exist as three persons? Should I love the Father, or the Son, or the Holy Spirit? If I prefer one to the others, will there be a conflict? Should I seek one over the others for help in specific problems?

Let me offer an inadequate explanation to the mystery of the love of God by writing about the concept of perfect oneness and unity in a Triune Person. God is present as three distinct Divine beings—

God the Father,
God the Son, and
God the Holy Spirit.

Yet, there is no polytheism, but monotheism. For, they are to be considered as only one 'Triune God' because of the spiritual closeness that binds them together. They do not have the limitation or need of separate physical bodies. The physical sensations have absolutely no place in this heavenly intimacy. But their love binds the three into one person. All I can understand is that God offers this binding love to us too.

1 John 5:7-8 *"For there are* ***three that bear record in heaven, the Father, the Word, and the Holy Ghost:*** *and* ***these three are one.*** *"*

God is unlike us, as He is Omnipotent [all powerful], omnipresent [He was present in the past, is in the present, and will be in the future] and omniscient [He sees and hears all things, knows all, namely the past, the present and the future happenings].

We cannot call God as our Father, unless the Father has a Son who is offering to make all those who are willing to be made joint heirs - children of God - with Him.

To present other analogies:

Oxygen is the energy – like the breath of God. Without O_2 on earth, there wouldn't be any fire. H_2O is water. Only the Living Water [Jesus Christ] can put out the fire of the holy God's justice and wrath [heat] because of the lust and sin of us the humans. But in a sense, the Living Water helps the fire of Love to burn brightly and steadily forever. When Potassium or Sodium is dropped into water, they start to burn.

You can see water as solid – when it is Ice
You can see it as liquid – when it is Water
You sense the vapor of it as hot steam, or
see it as cloud
Air has a mixture of Oxygen, Hydrogen, Nitrogen
and Carbon dioxide.
Air cannot be seen.
There are some who do not want believe what they
cannot see.
We cannot be (seen) without air.
You may see moisture or dust caught up in the air.
You may feel the wind blowing on you and around you.
You will know the wind entering and leaving your body,
if you are alive.
You never think about wind, till you are drowning, or
caught up in a cloud of smoke – or when your
airway is blocked. Some of us take God's love for
granted till we get short of breath, or, are
about to breathe our last.

Yet there are educated fools who say that there is no God because they cannot see or handle Him as a material object. These hooded educationalists, and self declared intellectuals who say they need concrete, tangible proof, talk about atom and teach about atoms and subatomic bodies - but have never ever seen a single atom in their lives! Yet not only do they believe in what they do not see or even feel, but they also teach others to believe their science.

THE ALPHABETICAL TYPES OF LOVE:

Apparent love
Bargaining love
Commanding love
Demanding love
Enduring love
Faulty love
Grudging love
Haughty love
Invincible love
Jesus (personification) love
Kind love
Liberating love
Mighty love
Never ending love
Outrageous love / Omnipotent love
Purging love
Quaking love / Quivering love/Quality love

Ritual love/ Raging love

Spontaneous love

Transparent love

Unfailing love

Violent love

Wondrous love

X-alting love

Yielding love

Zealous love

Chapter 8

Scriptures on Love

LOVE TOWARD GOD

1st Commandment

*Deut. 11:1: "You **must love the Lord your God and obey** all his requirements, laws, regulations, and commands".*

Joshua 22:5: "But be very careful to obey all the commands and the law that Moses gave to you. **Love the Lord your God**, walk in all his ways, obey his commands, be faithful to him, and serve him with all your heart and all your soul."

Matt. 22:38: "This is the **first and greatest commandment**".

Deut. 6:5: "And **you must love the Lord your God with all your heart, all your soul, and all your strength**".

Matt. 22:37: **Jesus replied, 'You must love the Lord your God with all your heart, all your soul, and all your mind.'**

Love is produced within us by-

The Holy Spirit

Gal 5:22: "But when the **Holy Spirit controls our lives, he will produce this kind of fruit in us: love, joy, peace, patience, kindness, goodness, faithfulness...**"

II Thes. 3:5: **"May the Lord bring you into an ever deeper understanding of the love of God and the endurance that comes from Christ"**.

God's love for us bounces back as echoes.

I John 4:19: **"We love each other as a result of his loving us first".**

Answer to prayer

Ps. 116:1: " I love the Lord because he hears and answers my prayers".

Can't love God without having love for people.

I John 4:10: "This is real love. It is not that we loved God, but that he loved us and sent his Son as a sacrifice to take away our sins".

Sacrifice without love to God is hypocrisy-

Luke 11:42: "But how terrible it will be for you Pharisees! For you are careful to tithe even the tiniest part of your income, but **you completely forget about justice and the love of God**. You should tithe, yes, but you should not leave undone the more important things".

John 5:42: "because I know **you don't have God's love within you**".

Your Love for God means you have Love for your neighbors.

The I & II commandments like a coin, have two sides – the head and the tail. Warping of one side will produce warping of the second, without fail.

How can we get this Love?

1. Your Love toward mankind is of God.

I John 4:7: " Dear friends**, let us continue to love one another, for love comes from God. Anyone who loves is born of God and knows God**".

This is God's II Great Command.

Matt. 37:39: ***"And the second is equally important: 'Love your neighbor as yourself'.***"

This Principle applies for the family also.

To our families:

Eph. 5:25: "And **you husbands must love your wives with the same love Christ showed the church. He gave up His life for her**".

Titus 2:4: "These older women ***must train the younger women to love their husbands and their children*****".**

Your love must be in Action also.

Gal. 6:10: " Whenever we have the opportunity, we should ***do good to everyone****, especially to our Christian brothers and sisters".*

Forgiving injuries.

Eph. 4:32: "Instead**, be kind to each other, tenderhearted, forgiving one another, just as God through Christ has forgiven you**"**.**

Col. 3:13: "**You must make allowance for each other's faults and forgive the person who offends you. Remember, the Lord forgave you, so you must forgive others**".

Luke 6:35 NIV "**But love your enemies, do good to them**, and lend to them without expecting to get anything back. Then your reward will be great, and you will be sons of the Most High, because he is kind to the ungrateful and wicked".

Romans 8:35-39.

"**Can anything ever separate us from Christ's love?** Does it mean he no longer loves us if we have trouble or calamity, or are persecuted, or are hungry or cold or in danger or threatened with death? [36] (Even the Scriptures say, "For your sake we are killed every day; we are being slaughtered like sheep.") [37] No, despite all these things, overwhelming victory is ours through Christ, who loved us".

The Greatest Promise of Love which God has made to us

Romans 8:35-39.

[38] **"And I am convinced that nothing can ever separate us from his love. Death can't, and life can't. The angels can't, and the demons can't. Our fears for today, our worries about tomorrow, and even the powers of hell can't keep God's love away. [39] Whether we are high above the sky or in the deepest ocean, nothing in all creation will ever be able to separate us from the love of God that is revealed in Christ Jesus our Lord".**

Chapter 9

LOVE and heartfelt RELATIONSHIP:

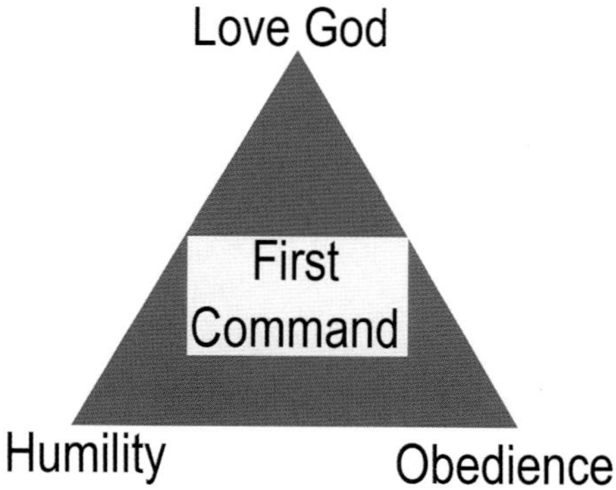

Our life is in our blood. Without oxygenation of our blood, we will be dead in five minutes. How do we get Oxygen into the blood? The red cells in our blood contain hemoglobin which gathers Oxygen from the air inhaled into the lungs. They also dump the waste product Carbon dioxide into the lungs which will be eliminated as we breathe out. The Oxygen is carried by the red cells to every part of the body through the arteries. The Oxygen is taken up by every cell in our body and exchanged with Carbon dioxide the waste product, which is carried back to the heart by the blood vessels called the veins. The inferior vena cava from the mid and lower body and the superior vena cava draining the upper part of the body are the largest veins. The veins dump the Oxygen depleted blood into the right side of the heart called the right-auricle.

The blood moves into the right ventricle through a valve. The valve prevents the blood from flowing back. From the right ventricle the blood is pumped by the heart into right and the left lungs. using the pulmonary artery, through the pulmonary valve. The pulmonary artery divides into the right and left to enter into the lungs. The blood is passed through tiny network of blood vessels called the capillaries surrounding the spongy expandable lung tissue. This is where the Oxygen is taken up and the Carbon dioxide given up by the red blood cells into the air in the lungs.

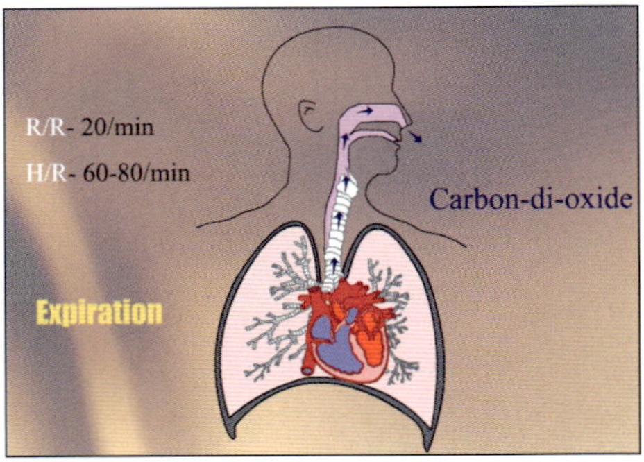

Repent, Confess, and get rid of sin

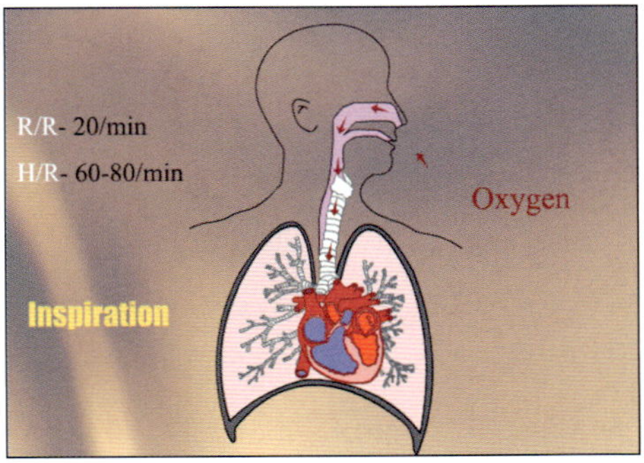

Get Jesus the Oxygen into heart & every red cell

Why are we given the 1st Commandment? Is God like us, starving to be loved? No, it is for our own sakes that He wants us to put Him first and love Him deeply. We really need to love God, if we plan to live with God in heaven on a 'long term' basis. For this, we need to be pardoned, and purified and be able to survive in a 'love' atmosphere.

The right Heart function is to connect us with God for forgiveness, purification and purpose.

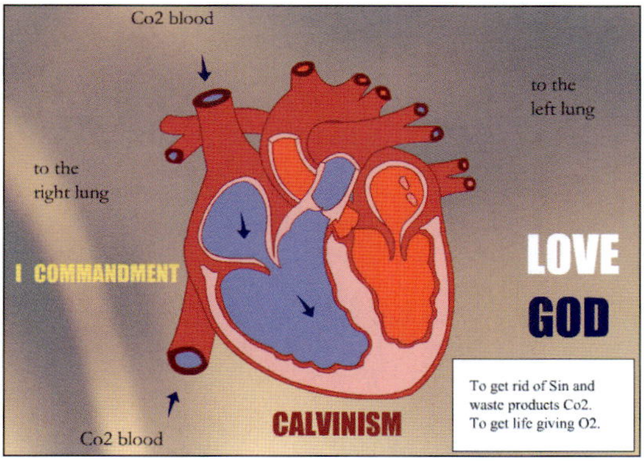

Right side of heart aims to get Oxygen into the blood after giving off impurities.

If the oxygenated clean blood that has been purified keeps on going between the right heart and the lungs, over and over, content to be cleaned and kept clean, the patient will die because of right heart failure. The oxygenated cleaned blood needs to be handed over to the left side of the heart, without retaining any blood for the right side.

The Right Heart: The right heart has to function right and receive the life essence Oxygen (Omega) from above through the act of inspiration into the lungs. And get rid of CO_2 – the corrupted 'self' expelled during the expiration, from the lungs.

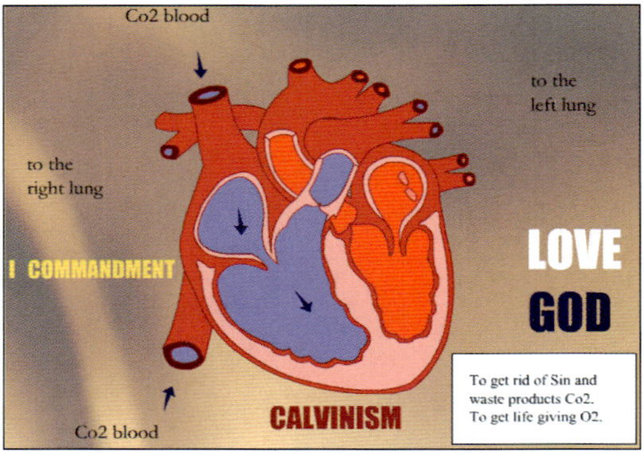

The 1st Commandment of Jesus:

To love your God with every thing in you
To receive His life – to be shared with others
To receive His word to be 'inspired'
To give up our 'self' by 'expiring' to self
To give up all bad things from the right heart
To give Him praise
To worship

Right heart receives impure blood to be cleaned up in the lungs.

The Right Heart is connected to the Left Heart.

The heart muscles work as one unit in unity and harmony.

Average 72 heart beats per minute.
Average 4 Respirations per minute.

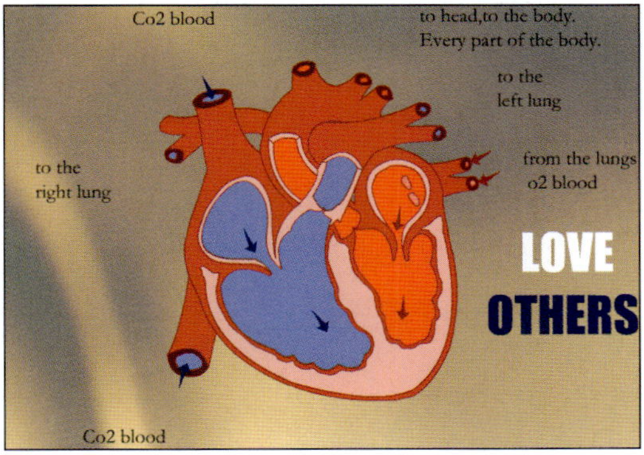

Your love for God is true, only when you can show love to others.

Relationship with lungs – inspirations: to receive God the Omega O_2, into the lungs.

Expiration –giving up the contaminations of the 'self'— CO_2.

The Left Heart function:

Relationship with various parts of the body – giving to others O_2 God's love.

To every minute cell in the body to share the life giving 'O_2' unceasingly.

Through the aorta, major arteries smaller arteriole, and capillaries.

The garbage is collected [gathered up] by the blood through the tiny-venules, larger veins, the inferior and the superior vena cava to be delivered into the right auricle on the Right side of the heart, so that the blood may be sent to lungs for the cleansing of CO_2 and filling in with O_2.

Love for God takes you to Him–for cleansing, the venous blood – 1st Command.

Love of Others through God – to give oxygenated blood to others – 2nd Command.

The Left Heart:

The 2nd Commandments of Jesus
is, 'to love our neighbors'
And, 'to serve our neighbors'.

Unless the right heart has done its work, the left heart cannot function, nor be of any use.

The 2nd Commandment: To love the neighbors means we should live to share God's love with others - caring, sharing, bringing and enjoying heaven even in our short term stay on earth. God's love manifested for one another on earth is the 2nd commandment.

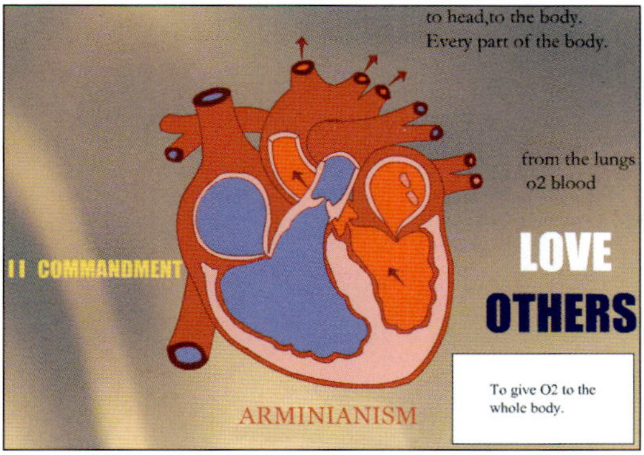

The left ventricle empties itself completely into the Aorta, the artery supplying the whole body. The left auricle receives the oxygenated, purified, hemoglobin rich blood and passes it down to the left ventricle. The left ventricle squeezes out every drop of the rich blood into the aorta; any back flow is prevented by the Aortic valve. Aorta, the big artery going out of the heart gives branches to the head, arms, chest, abdomen, pelvis, lower limbs - in short to every part of the body. If the left ventricle tries to retain some of the rich blood for itself, this will result in left heart failure. The lungs will be filled with fluid and blood and drown the patient to death.

Prayer is comparable to the craving of an empty heart.

Praise is comparable to the moving of life [blood] from the right heart into the right and left lungs.

Worship is comparable to the propulsion our life [blood] the left heart to supply the entire body.

If you love others, you will care for them and share with them the good things you have. It is not only good for you, it also safeguards you.

There are no boundaries or fences or walls for the love of God. On earth if you say you love your neighbor – check if there is any boundary that limits it in various forms of 'self'.

Immediate family, blood relatives, same caste or community, color or nationality or church or denomination, the one who agrees with you in some way: these are all walls and boundaries. If what you have is limited and contained within these boundaries, - what you have is not love. Ask God to shine His light upon it and let you know what kind of substitute poison it is!

Love is the atmosphere of Heaven. God wants you to enjoy it on earth – while you are alive on earth – as well as in Heaven. God's love could not even be contained in the heavens. That is why He came down to earth, so that you could enjoy His love on earth as well. If what you breathe and convey is not love, you will not survive in heaven. If you get used to breathing hell's fumes and get comfortable and adapted to it, you are in danger of ending up there.

There is no geographic boundary for a Christian, nor is there a limited linkage caused by blood or genes. The family for a Christian is his or her neighbor who is in need!

Chapter 10

Terrestrial Love compared with Celestial :

Galatians 5:19-21 (NLT) "When you follow the desires of your sinful nature, your lives will produce these evil results: sexual immorality, impure thoughts, eagerness for lustful pleasure, [20] idolatry, participation in demonic activities, hostility, quarreling, jealousy, outbursts of anger, selfish ambition, divisions, the feeling that everyone is wrong except those in your own little group, [21] envy, drunkenness, wild parties, and other kinds of sin. Let me tell you again, as I have before, that anyone living that sort of life will not inherit the Kingdom of God."

Many humans love the following and think it is okay:

Impure thoughts, eagerness for lustful pleasure, idolatry, spiritism, hatred and fighting, jealousy, anger, constant effort to get the best for yourself, complaints, criticism, the feeling that everyone else is wrong, wrong doctrine, envy, murder, drunkenness, wild parties.

Celestial love [Charity]

Galatians 5:22-23: "But when the Holy Spirit controls our lives, He will produce this kind of fruit in us: love, joy, peace, patience, kindness, goodness, faithfulness, [23] gentleness, and self-control. Here there is no conflict with the law."

True Love keeps you from not being a

Man pleaser
Woman pleaser
Child pleaser
Boss pleaser
Officer Pleaser
President Pleaser
Society pleaser
Self pleaser
People pleaser

All the above take you into terrestrial, self centered love

But being a GOD pleaser, takes you to Celestial love.

(We may recognize that the Great Commission is to enable us to put into action our love for our neighbors. People may go on such missions, but should not forget to take the 2nd Commandment – LOVE - with them. Otherwise, they will be like lamps without oil, or guns without ammunition).

Chapter 11

LASTING LOVE:

Please God, into me put Thy love
So that, only for Thee, I will live.

What gets many Christians' attention is the great commission
While strangely the second commandment suffers a sad omission.

Matt. 28:19-20: "Therefore, go and make disciples of all the nations, baptizing them in the name of the Father and the Son and the Holy Spirit. [20] ***Teach these new disciples to obey all the commands I have given you****. And be sure of this: I am with you always, even to the end of the age."*

Matt.22:37-40: **Jesus replied, " 'You must love the Lord your God with all your heart, all your soul, and all your mind.' [38] This is the first and greatest commandment. [39] A second is equally important: 'Love your neighbor as yourself.'** [40] All the other commandments and all the demands of the prophets are based on these two commandments."

Your capacity for God's love will only grow
If often, upon your knees you humbly bow.

Sometimes Jesus asked people when he healed or brought them out from the dead. e.g.- Jairus' daughter, not to talk about it [the spectacular miracle] but to give thanks to God and get closer to Him first. For, talking with others even about good and great things dilutes us and takes us away from the one who did the wonder [God]; we tend to become show–offs ourselves. One exception was the man possessed by a legion of evil spirits. After his healing he was asked by Jesus to stay back and witness for Jesus in a hostile place that did not want Jesus to stay to help the local people.

EXPRESSIONS:

We are taught by many, to express well our lust
But are shy and silent, to express our love and trust.

Love – knocks down walls.
Love – builds new bridges.
Love – builds Dams.
Love – salvages the Damned.
Love – finds a way through wilderness.
Love – says 'No way' to despair.
Love – sends strong ripples on the surface.

Love – sends strong currents in the deep.
Love – listens, even to a bore.
Love - lingers with the forlorn.
Love – anticipates – loved ones' return.
Love – participates in union.
Love – does not cover up.
Love - is transparent.
Love - is truthful. There is no place for lie.
Love – liberates – Truth sets you free.
Love – dies out of, and for love – but yet lives on for ever.
Love – believes.
Love – acts out the Beatitudes.

THE TEN commandments-QUALITIES OF LOVE

Love will make you

1. Care – and be kind to others
2. Bear – the cross whatever be the cost
3. Share – not be 'selfish', but be giving
4. Wear – humility, not be haughty
5. Fair – not to be glad about injustice – but rejoice in truth and in God's will
6. Cure – your spiritual, emotional and physical illness
7. Endure – Trials and Tribulations and Persecutions
8. Procure – God's blessings on others
9. Secure – Eternal life
10. Obscure – Self and self interest

Chapter 12

Love sonnets to place under our bonnets

1. **How true**

   If what I have I don't share,
   It is because I don't care.
   What is not present in the pot?
   Cannot, out in a spoon be brought.

2. **Divine principle**

   When our hearts are ruled by God's loving,
   Giving and serving will become our way of living.

3. **Expect to receive**

   When at God's love you do thrill,
   The same God's love will you fill.

4. **Let it out**

   Lasting loving good will come out of you,
   When all deep selfishness goes out of you.

5. **Your exclamation**

   When your heart is a bad pump,
   Evil from your mouth can jump.

6. **Remember Solomon**

   Human wisdom perverts,
   God's love converts.

7. **Possessive love**

When your love is possessive,
Your self-demands get aggressive.

8. **Loves apparel**

Love bears everything but hurt and grudge,
Love cares and on self, does not indulge.

9. **Emotion is a commotion**

Possessive human love is all too brief,
And in its wake brings too much grief.

10. **Get reconditioned**

Take, Lord, away from me conditional love,
Fill me, Lord with Thy unconditional love.

11. **Com(e)-passion**

Lord, let all my mortal passion,
Be tempered with Thy compassion.

12. **Long (distance) suffering**

Godly love forbears and endures long-suffering;
Phone gossip ups fares in long-distance 'sharing'.

13. **Love links**

Love doesn't just make you like or kindly think,
But, love you to the other will strongly link.

14. **My desire**

When God's love you desire,
He will set your heart on holy fire.

15. That's for sure

If you fall in love for the wrong reason,
You will one day face strong treason.

16. Pour-over

When at God's feet your life you pour,
On earth and heaven your spirit will soar.

17. No partition

When you learn to pray and God adore,
Between you and God, there won't be a door.

18. Passion or Compassion?

Zeal and passion tend to lead us into anger,
It is for Godly compassion we need to hunger.

19. Gloat not

Lord, let me never ever gloat,
When one I dislike falls off a boat.
Help me Lord, to learn to love that one
Knowing that he is loved by Thee.
Let me Lord, from self be free.

20. Aetiology of ailment

If your love for good and God is ailing,
It is because your Bible reading is trailing.

21. Oh for some resemblance

Within my heart I confess Thee as Father God,
With my lips profess Thee as Sovereign God
and Lord.

Yet in me I see hardly a likeness of the Lord,
Who because of love bore the cross for me
May the time soon come when I may look
like Thee,
For others to see, and like me, receive Thee.

22. Do not prolong Love's suffering

Just don't give love a long time suffering,
Or, recurrent, intermittent, minor suffering.

23. Terrestrial or celestial?

Love that turns to anger and withdrawal
is terrestrial;
Love that endures on with concern and prayer,
is celestial.

24. Ultimate freedom

When you have learned to love truly,
You have then learned to live freely.

25. Saving face

When you learn to love others through His grace,
You will never ever suffer from any disgrace.

26. What matters and what not

It matters not how much you do
It matters not how well you do
It matters, though, how much love you have
for those in want,
For that decides what matters and what doesn't.

27. A farce has no force

To give without loving,
Or love without giving,
Are both exercises in futility?
For, they both have no lasting utility.

28. Love is a levelling shovel

If you find your moods often swell and shrivel,
Love is the shovel that can make an even level.

29. Love to live - live to love

Start within me for Thee a great and growing love,
That I may with Thee, and for Thee, joyfully live.

30. Phoenix in ashes: ashes don't raise Phoenix

Grant me, Lord, to love others while living,
And not to be given to, any belated grieving.
Let me not build Tajmahals or memorials colossus,
Nor shed my tears over tombs of people or
lost causes,
Teach me Lord, to fully love and live each day,
And not run my fingers to find things in ashes
of yesterday.

31. Buy the "bonds" that bonds and holds

Most painful loss is a loved one's separation,
For which each one of us needs preparation,
And pray for "stretch" of bonds of love,
To keep with ones who 'fore us go above.

This by our puny human efforts is impossible,
But by God's "savings-bond" is now possible.

32. Let peace increase

Teach us oh God, to live in peace
And with those we love to be at ease.
Knowing soon our gatherings will decrease,
For one by one we all decease.

33. Guard against fraud

Lord, let me no more with words or
actions pretend,
But with Thy love, to other's need
prayerfully attend.

34. Tax does taste like wax

Any one can be persuaded to give-in to pruning
But it takes godly love to delight in selfless giving.

35. Desire is a fire

Lord, let me constantly burn with a
holy unquenchable desire
For Thy Spirit to share the gospel, set me on fire.

36. Love takes "U" above lust

Love whenever spent, strengthens
But lust alas, only repels and weakens.

37. Echoes in the ghettos

When Thy message to me by grace is spoken,

Let me not like a rock, just pass the echoes.
But rather let my hardened heart be broken,
And multiply Thy message into manifold re-echoes.

38. Stream through this rock

Speak, oh Lord to my heart today
To start a flow of Thy love I pray
A flow that never, never dries
But as an unfailing fountain does ever flow.

39. Let the Son rise upon the ice

Often my heart is cold as ice
May Thy loving warmth make it otherwise
Let the Son of God in my heart arise
And steam it turn, for thy service raise.

40. Lasting help for the lost

In unceasing prayer prevail
For love to last, travail.

41. Child's love

Teach me Lord to love Thee
Every time I meet Thee
To greet Thee and fly into Thy arms
And stay there safe from all that harms.

42. Warm love

Like butter near a flame may my heart melt
And my love for Thee be always heart felt.

43. First love

May my heart throb, and my pulse race,
Every time I see Thy tender loving face.

44. Bonding love

Let my knees buckle and to the ground drop
While my breath labours and does desperately gasp
Yearning to be bound by Thy heavenly rope
And stay yielded and still in Thy loving grasp.

45. Selfless love

May my self be lost, and there be no more 'I'
And from all things self, to Thee fly,
May my 'I' be bent to 'C' for Christ,
That He alone 'll be my soul's delight.

46. Without love, need CPR

If I don't to Thee thus respond
Please do on me Thy CPR
That I be filled with Thy breath
May that be my only inspiration
And gratitude and love my expiration
Let my whole and soul for Thee, ache
All my self and pride, off-me do take.

47. Into me see and establish intimacy

Lord I often act as a religious Pharisee,
Who knows not that from God, "far is he",
Give me grace Lord for me to see,
And from the evil within me, to Thee flee

And by Thy grace please set me free
To enjoy with Thee eternal intimacy.

48. Respiration without perspiration

When my inspiration becomes Thy breath 'in-me' attitude
My expiration can then become a prayer of gratitude.

49. All for Alpha

When for God's love and company you start aching,
That is the beginning of your life's making.

50. A stony heart

I seem to have a heart of stone
A hard round desiccated stone
Holding within no softness or moisture
Mercy showers notwithstanding quiet alone,
Retaining no water, nor fit for pasture.

51. Stricken stone

Speak oh Lord to this hardened stone,
Use me as witness for the One who does atone
Let there be a constant flow of Thy stream
In service of the one who came to redeem.

52. Bare love, don't bear-hug

Let not your expressions in hugs of love,
People's ribs painfully break

Nor choke or suffocate as you show your love
Or cause bones to break by your hearty
hand-shake.

53. Old is to hold

A mother and her love can never get too old,
For she becomes dearer and dearer to hold.

54. Laundering the light

If for God's love you don't act as a reflector,
You may end-up as His light's deflector.

55. To be or not to be

To love is to serve, even the undeserved,
To be loved is to be unconditionally served.

56. What you own, lets you down

When you reckon your loved ones,
Do not to your expectation measure-up
Don't shrink away, or them in anyway shun,
With prayer to God, do lift them up.

57. Write on the 'heart-drive'

Please write Thy laws upon my heart,
Never let me from these depart.

58. CPU will bless you

May my every heart-beat,
Carry on to each and every cell,
Thy holy word to soak and treat,

And all my warring 'discords' quell.
May Thy message then to my mouth jump,
And Thy living waters to others, pump.

59. Don't go reeling, get a healing

Human love is limited by the sense of feeling,
God's love covers our body, mind and soul with
wholesome healing.

60. Live in love

Please God, within me put Thy Love, .
And let me for Thee always live.

61. It is that simple

You become God's disciple,
When you love and live the Bible.

62. The sheep's voice

The love of God will tenderly gather together
All those who from their hearts call Him
Abba Father.

63. Love-Links

When we really become (thro' God's love) one
with the Father
Holy love springs on earth between one another.

64. Eureka

When you find with God, a new relation
You have just become a new Christian

65. Unchanging

Nothing holy I ever do
Will make God love me more
Nothing bad I ever do
Will make God love me less or no more.

66. Supply from high

God, He will supply all our needs
When we share with others thro' our deeds.

67. Don't carry or convey

When you have a severe infection,
Your kisses become deadly deception.

68. Lasting Love

Please God, within me put Thy love,
That for Thee I'll live here and above.

69. Not seasonal

Let not my love for thee be seasonal
Or like the division of each day-diurnal
Nor like the woman's ovulational or emotional;
But be constant, and at all times devotional.

70. To even flow

Let not my love for thee be a pulsed flow,
With a rise and fall of every heart squeeze,
But flow with a steady stream, here below,
And feed the baby Christians, bringing peace.

71. Not flashing light, but flash light

Let my love for thee not flicker,
Like an oil lamp, with only the wicker,
Nor let it pulse and flash like a strobe,
But glow steadily while I live on this globe.

72. No diminuendo

Let my love for Thee be an ever-rising crescendo,
And not become diminuendo or fluctuating tremolo.

73. Ultimate demand

Human love can give some blood in transfusion,
Divine love wholly yielded the Son for our
salvation.

(John 3:16 NIV) "For God so loved the world that he gave his one and only Son, that whoever believes in him shall not perish but have eternal life.

74. Love does not promote

Agape love does not ignore, nor does any sinful
indulgence support,
But will correct, and to restore heavenly harmony
make every effort.

(1 John 1:6-7 NIV) If we claim to have fellowship with him yet walk in the darkness, we lie and do not live by the truth. But if we walk in the light,

as he is in the light, we have fellowship with one another, and the blood of Jesus, his Son, purifies us from all sin.

75. Soul's desire

Let our sole desire be to love and serve
And from Thy will and path, never swerve

76. This is not love

Sadly, every living earthly organism,
Looses its love, after a lusty orgasm.

77. Celestial

What is the definition of love?
That, which comes from above.

78. Divine Digitalis

Be thankful to God, no matter what,
That is what God wants in your heart.

1Thess 5:15-18

79. Heart transplant

A grateful heart from God's heaven is sent,
This keeps your coronaries open as with a Stent.

Ezek. 36:26-27

80. Pillar of cloud by day & Pillar of light by night

Love and obey God's commandments during
the day,

With songs of psalms and thanksgiving, at night
do pray.

81. Dumping syndrome

Let not our (loving) handout,
Tear, or wear the others – out.

(e.g. cooking food, gifts, baby - sitting, home-sitting, labour distribution - etc. should be done with a heart to help - not overwhelm, imitate, or intimidate others. These are delicate services - like the buoyancy of the water in the river that holds and supports the boat.)

82. Please the Father

A child loves the father, yet fears him for his
correctional punishment,
A Christian loves the Father, and fears to hurt Him
by his accomplishment.

83. Not to beg - but hug

Don't become a Christian - just from God to ask,
Be some one ready to serve, and in His love to
bask.

84. Offensive self

Out of love for man, God, His son, He sent,
Out of love for our 'selves', others we resent.

85. Love feast not lust beast!

God, He gave 'love' to be holy and spiritual,
Man has turned it into a bad, selfish victual.

86. Wretched man that I am

When I profess and confess, "My God I love Thee",
How is it there is no love for my neighbour
within me?

87. Commandments-1&2

Loving God is to breathe Him in, with each
inspiration,
Loving neighbours, is to die to self and is called
expiration.

88. True Love

When you really love one-another,
Covetousness leaves you altogether.

89. Breeze for my wheeze!

May my deep love and longing for Thee,
Like the drowning man's need for air be.

90. Asthmatic

Sin, like carbonated air in the lungs of an
asthmatic,
Does not leave by his efforts desperate
and frantic.

91. Let-out

Let my each and every respiration,
Cause my sins, expiration.

92. Longing

Give me Lord a deep and earnest anticipation,
For Thy presence in my prayer, participation.

93. Labour lost without love

Let not your ambition be, to be 'doing',
But by yielding to and in Him, 'being'.

94. Forget your'self'

In God's service,
May there be no 'self' awareness,
Let it suffice,
To be aware only of His nearness.

95. Bubble has trouble

If your love is mixed with lust,
It can ferment and easily burst.

96. Meekness is not weakness

When in appearance, Christ's love in you
makes you vulnerable,
You are not really weak but strong in God who
indeed is venerable.

97. The seeker and solicitor!

God after man is ever the loving seeker,
Jesus in defence of man is ever the Speaker.

98. Initiative

After Adam disobeyed, and into sin did fall,
It was God who pursued him, lifted up His voice to call.

99. Shape of Love

When you allow God's love to break you,
His great love will mould and make you.

100. Air Hunger

May my need for Thee make me gulp and grasp,
Like a drowning person's need for air to gasp.

101. Can't out-give God

I thought for God's sake I gave up my many pleasures,
Little did I know that on me, He heaps great treasures.

102. Get in Pace for the Great Race

When we all with God, get into good rhythm,
Our lives will flow in heaven's "algo" rhythm.

103. When 1st Commandment is "IN", 2nd is "OUT"!

Fill me with love for Thee,
May this love grow deep within,
Flood me with love from Thee,
To flow to others from within.

104. Can't buy love with

To win love, you can't use force or power,
Nor avail of any permissive 'shower'.

105. Two Come After One

You can't keep or follow the second commandment,
Till you understand and keep the first
commandment.

106. Love Claim

The grace of God came down as love upon earth,
And staked its 'claim' with the Saviour's death.

107. What is grace?

The blend of mercy, pity and love on God's
holy face,
Is what can inadequately be labeled "amazing
grace".

108. Child Like

Children call their loved ones to play,
Let me call on my loving Lord and pray.

109. My goal

Let me at your feet, in love, be basking,
And for my own self, nothing be asking.

110. Love or lust

God gave pure love to mankind as a priceless
present,

But man twists love to lust with devil's help,
at present.

111. Love your enemies

To love our enemy is not a simple suggestion,
It is a command you better take-in for digestion.

112. Charity

When you downgrade the value of chastity
You have sin in you, and no Godly charity
For God's standard of charity is interwoven
with purity.

113. Cords of love

Love is not "had to"
Love is "can't but do"

114. Miser inside

If you're not the giving sort
Look inside, to see why not.

115. Long sufferance

Love is not to be put to test and needless use
Like a fruit that needs to be squeezed for
the juice.

116. Sour love

If your love has not become sweet and ripe
Anyone biting or tasting you will surely gripe.

117. Heart sounds-'Luv-Dub'

Let my every heart beat sound 'I love God'
And every cardiac output pour to others the
love of God.

118. Love-light

Giving willingly to the needy is 'turning on' the light
Don't treat this celestial matter light or with spite.

119. More like the Master

When you become more like Jesus,
You love and give 'self' away like Jesus.

120. What a giving

Love is ever, for, giving
Love forever is forgiving.

121. Love's pulse

May our hearts with love for God and others pulse
Let not our hearts, other humans or God, repulse.

122. Love

If in your life, you don't have God's love,
You cannot with Him live, here or above.

123. Spelling mistakes, which affect our stakes

When the letter 'L' for Love gets into wrong
places in your life:-
"Love for God" changes to "love for go[l]d"

"Love for Word" changes to "love for wor[l]d"
Wanting "God to save us" changes to "gold
to enslave us".

124. Love's labor lost

Let not my love, or care for those in the family
Cause any discord or division in the family.

125. Love one another

Lord you are the maker and the giver,
You made us and gave us one to another.

126. Sympathy & Empathy

Out of kindness to others, at their troubles
you sympathize,
Out of love, you will in agony with them,
empathize.

127. Heart-throb

May our hearts with God's love, pulse,
In our hearts let us not others repulse

128. Miss-spelt

You may preach your love for God,
But it may spell out as love for Gold.

129. Hope, faith and love

Fear, with reverence for God will develop into Hope
Faith can develop into walk of trust and hope
Enabling us not just love to live, but live with love
from above.

130. Faith, Hope, Love and Grace-alive

Grant me Thy Grace, and
Deep Faith to honor Thee,
Hope and Trust to please Thee,
Love and Charity, to live for Thee.

131. Compassionate

In your Christian life, is there any real passion?
In your heart and life is there godly compassion?

132. Passionate

Where there is great passion,
There is no room for caution.

133. Luke-warm, look-worm

When any Christian, for gospel, develops apathy,
He bids farewell to his basic sympathy and
empathy.

134. Unearth, earth

God wants us to love and live with those on earth,
Once, from us and others He does all sins unearth.

135. Compare and contrast

God longs to hug humanity,
That is the love of Divinity.
We hug our 'selves' in vanity,
Is that not an absurd insanity?

136. Difference between Prayer and Worship

Prayer is the longing of an empty heart in 'diastole',
Worship is the overflowing of the filled heart in 'systole'.

137. Chasing Love

His love's mission is to keep you from the lion's jaws,
Or drink the lethal potion, which the world from hell draws.

138. Love's Heart-beat

May my total Passion for God from my Right Heart,
Match godly compassion for others from my Left Heart.

Chapter 13

Love leads to intimacy and transparency.
Bible references:

THE INTIMACY BETWEEN THE FATHER AND JESUS is like the Right and the Left sides of the heart, the four chambered single Heart of the Triune God.

Matt. 3:17: And a voice from heaven said, "This is my beloved Son, and I am fully pleased with him."

Mark. 1:11: And a voice came from heaven saying, "You are my beloved Son, and I am fully pleased with you."

Luke 3:22: And the Holy Spirit descended on him in the form of a dove. And a voice from heaven said, "You are my beloved Son, and I am fully pleased with you."

John 17:23, 26: "I in them and you in me, all being perfected into one. Then the world will know that you sent me and will understand that you love them as much as you love me. [24] Father... you gave me the glory because you loved me even before the world began! [26] And I have revealed you to them and will keep on revealing you. I will do this so that your love for me may be in them and I in them."

Matt.17:5: But even as he said it, a bright cloud came over them, and a voice from the cloud said, "This is my beloved Son, and I am fully pleased with him. Listen to him."

Mk. 9:7; Lk.9:35; 2 Peter 1:17: And he received honor and glory from God the Father when God's glorious, majestic voice called down from heaven, "This is my beloved Son; I am fully pleased with him."

John 17:24: Thou lovest me before the foundation of the world.

John 10:17: The Father loves me because I lay down my life that I may have it back again.

John 3:35: The Father loves his Son, and he has given him authority over everything.

John 5:20: For the Father loves the Son and tells him everything he is doing, and the Son will do far greater things than healing this man.

John 15:9: I have loved you even as the Father has loved me. Remain in my love.

GOD'S GREAT LOVE FOR US, HIS UNWORTHY CREATION.

John 3:16: "For God so loved the world that he gave his only Son, so that everyone who believes in him will not perish but have eternal life.

God is offering and inviting us into sharing the intimacy between Him and Jesus, and be included into the intimacy between the Holy Trinity.

Chapter 14

Truth can set us free. WHEN?

What the Bible says:

The truth contains wisdom and knowledge. But the truth has to be "understood" to be obeyed and that is possible when we willingly "stand-under" Him. This is what Jesus did as He stood-under the will of the Father at all times. God wants us to apply this principle and "stand-under" Him, which is to say, obey Him and continue in His presence.

God's presence is God's will; if you leave God's presence, you go out of God's will.

What is truth ?

God is truth. We need to believe and walk in this light. Love is the light which shines on His way. We should obey the road rules all the way – (not be wayward).

Love is the Truth, the Life, and the Way. This love fuels our vehicles. This love is also the bread to nourish us. This love is the living water, the drink for us which flows from our bellies to others to enable others to come to the Creator, the Savior, the Spirit and the source of all that is good, godly, and all power.

My grand child Joanna who when 5 years old, composed the following:-

Words and writing can be erased away,

But God's Love is here, always to stay.

Liberal views

Lack of love and concern will make you a hypocritical liberal,

Would you dare to speak the truth with love, even if charged with libel?

Love a power
Power without God's love in one is a calamity,
Love without power does not exist as an entity.
Love has to be acted out in our daily life.

1 John 3:17-18: "But **if anyone has enough money to live well and sees a brother or sister in need and refuses to help—how can God's love be in that person?**

Love is not lip service

[18] Dear children, **let us stop just saying we love each other; let us really show it by our actions.**"

Love is being generous

1 Peter 4:10: "God has given gifts to each of you from his great variety of spiritual gifts. Manage them well ***so that God's generosity can flow through you.****"*

Love is to be tender and humble

1 Peter 3:8: "Finally, all of you should be of one mind, full of sympathy toward each other, **loving one another with tender hearts and humble minds.**"

Love binds our hearts together

Philip. 2:1-11: Is there any encouragement from belonging to Christ? Any comfort from his love? Any fellowship together in the Spirit? Are your hearts tender and sympathetic? [2] Then make me truly happy by agreeing wholeheartedly with each other, **loving one another, and working together with one heart and purpose.**

Love considers and places others before self

[3] Don't be selfish; don't live to make a good impression on others. **Be humble, thinking of others as better than yourself.** [4] Don't think only about your own affairs, but be interested in others too, and what they are doing.

Love is the attitude of mind which Jesus had

[5] **Your attitude should be the same that Christ Jesus had**. [6] **Though he was God, he did not demand and cling to his rights as God.** [7] **He made himself nothing; he took the humble position of a slave and appeared in human form**. [8] **And in human form he obediently humbled himself even further by dying a criminal's death on a cross.**

Love makes us tender and forgiving

Ephes. 4:32: "Instead, **be kind to each other, tenderhearted, forgiving one another, just as God through Christ has forgiven you**."

The true freedom is to serve others with love

Galatians 5:13: "For you have been called to live in freedom—not freedom to satisfy your sinful nature, but **freedom to serve one another in love**."

Love gives with joy

2 Cor. 9:7: "You must each make up your own mind as to how much you should give. **Don't give reluctantly or in response to pressure**. For God loves the person who **gives cheerfully.**"

The most comfortable love

2 Cor. 1:3-4: "All praise to the God and Father of our Lord Jesus Christ. He is the source of every mercy and the God who comforts us. [4] **He comforts us in all our troubles so that we can comfort others.** When others are troubled, we will be able to give them the same comfort God has given us."

Love your neighbor

Luke 10:30-37: Jesus replied with an illustration: "A Jewish man was traveling on a trip from Jerusalem to Jericho, and he was attacked by bandits. They stripped him of his clothes and money, beat him up, and left him half dead beside the road.

[31] "By chance a Jewish priest came along; but when he saw the man lying there, he crossed to the other side of the road and passed him by. [32] A Temple assistant walked over and looked at him lying there, but he also passed by on the other side.

[33] "Then a despised Samaritan came along, and when he saw the man, he felt deep pity. [34] Kneeling beside him, the Samaritan soothed his wounds with medicine and bandaged them. Then he put the man on his own donkey and took him to an inn, where he took care of him. [35] The next day he handed the innkeeper two pieces

of silver and told him to take care of the man. 'If his bill runs higher than that,' he said, 'I'll pay the difference the next time I am here.'

[36] "**Now which of these three would you say was a neighbor to the man who was attacked by bandits?" Jesus asked**.

[37] The man replied, "**The one who showed him mercy**."

Then Jesus said, "Yes, now **go and do the same**."

When you give love to humans you will receive love from God

Luke 6:38: "**If you give, you will receive**. Your gift will return to you in full measure, pressed down, shaken together to make room for more, and running over. Whatever measure you use in giving—large or small—it will be used to measure what is given back to you."

Like love and lust are not the same, sheep and goats are different.

Matthew 25:31-46: "But when the Son of Man comes in his glory, and all the angels with him, then he will sit upon his glorious throne. [32] All the nations will be gathered in his presence, **and he will separate them as a shepherd separates the sheep from the goats**.

[33] He will place the sheep at his right hand and the goats at his left.

For a casual observer, the sheep and the goat may appear to be the same. But the Shepherd knows the difference.

[34] "Then the King will say to those on the right, 'Come, you who are blessed by my Father, inherit the Kingdom prepared for you from the foundation of the world. [35] For I was hungry, and **you fed me**. I was thirsty, and **you gave me a drink**. I was a stranger, and **you invited me into your home.** [36] I was naked, and **you gave me clothing**. I was sick, and **you cared for me**. I was in prison, and **you visited me**.'

The children of God are not even aware of the fact that the Lord has worked through them. They didn't show the love of God to others, in order to be recognized.

[37] "Then these righteous ones will reply, 'Lord, when did we ever see you hungry and feed you? Or thirsty and give you something to drink? [38] Or a stranger and show you hospitality? Or naked and give you clothing? [39] When did we ever see you sick or in prison, and visit you?' [40] And **the King will tell them**, 'I assure you, **when you did it to one of the least of these my brothers and sisters, you were doing it to me!**'

[41] "Then the King will turn to those on the left and say, 'Away with you, you cursed ones, into the eternal fire prepared for the Devil and his demons! [42] For I was hungry, and you didn't feed me. I was thirsty, and you didn't give me anything to drink. [43] I was a stranger, and you didn't invite me into your home. I was naked, and you gave me no clothing. I was sick and in prison, and you didn't visit me.'

Those who have an ulterior motive in pleasing the Lord would choose the right opportunities and occasions to serve God. Though they heard what God told the sheep on the right side.

[44] " they will reply, 'Lord, when did we ever see you hungry or thirsty or a stranger or naked or sick or in prison, and not help you?' [45] And he will answer, 'I assure you, when you refused to help the least of these my brothers and sisters; you were refusing to help me.' [46] And they will go away into eternal punishment, but the righteous will go into eternal life."

Love, willingly becomes the lowly servant

Matthew 20:25-28: But Jesus called them together and said, "You know that in this world kings are tyrants, and officials lord it over the people beneath them. [26] But among you it should be quite different. **Whoever wants to be a leader among you must be your servant,**

[27] and whoever wants to be first must become your slave. [28] For **even I, the Son of Man, came here not to be served but to serve others, and to give my life as a ransom for many.**"

Love in Action

Isaiah 58:7-10: "I want you to **share your food with the hungry** and to **welcome poor wanderers into your homes. Give clothes to those who need them, and do not hide from relatives who need your help.**

[8] "**If you do these things**, your salvation will come like the dawn**. Yes, your healing will come quickly. Your godliness will lead you forward, and the glory of the Lord will protect you from behind**. [9] Then when you call, the Lord will answer. 'Yes, I am here,' he will quickly reply.

"***Stop oppressing the helpless and stop making false accusations and spreading vicious rumors! [10] Feed the hungry and help those in trouble. Then your light will shine out from the darkness, and the darkness around you will be as bright as day.***"

Do not attempt a calculated bribery, as service to God

Proverbs 18:16: "Giving a gift works wonders; it may bring **you** before important people!"

If you are godly, you will not ill treat any other human, whatever is their color, creed or status. There should be no slavery, whether open or covert.

Proverbs 12:10 The godly are concerned for the welfare of their animals, but ***even the kindness of the wicked is cruel.***

Love heals

Matthew 14:14 A vast crowd was there as he stepped from the boat, and he **had compassion on them and healed their sick.**

Mark 1:41 **Moved with pity**, Jesus touched him. "I want to," he said. "**Be healed**!"

God's love which the heaven could not contain and which overflowed down to earth:—

John 3:16 **"For God so loved the world that he gave his only Son, so that everyone who believes in him will not perish but have eternal life."**

Chapter 15

1 Corinthians Chapter 13

The 13th chapter of the First Corinthians may be considered as the vehicle offered for us in our journey to Heaven. Whether we want to or not, we all have to take the Hi-way to Heaven, or to Hell. It is best to take the one offered to us by God, for our travel and destination will be covered by Heavenly Insurance.

The first four verses of the chapter are like the four comfortable adjustable chairs in the vehicle. The Steering wheel is the free will [wheel] God has given to us. Thus the choice of direction is given to us. But the vehicle cannot move yet. The designer God's engine will have to be put under the hood or the bonnet of the vehicle.

The Gas tank will have to be installed and filled up.The body of the car or the Chassis is the Lord Jesus who bridges the Engine [The Creator], the Gas tank [Power through the Holy Spirit] and us to carry us in good seats by laying His life and body 'aCross', under us as a support.

Here is a diagrammatic representation.

FOUR GREATEST ACHIEVEMENTS POSSIBLE, WITHOUT HAVING LOVE!

Gift of **Communication** in all the languages of Earth. There are over 5000 languages on earth.And of Heavens - all of heavens!! To Speak - without time spent to learn!1.Cor.13: 1	Gift of **Prophesy**; wisdom and knowledge of past, present and future. In every thing there is to know where treasures are, where oil is - where danger is and how to prevent it?1.Cor.13: 2
Gift of **Faith**. Performing miracles, healing, and wonders Make Objects and obstacles to move.1.Cor.13: 2	Gift of **Service** and **self sacrifice** to others - **Give up** time, **all** possessions and even be burnt alive, for preaching and suffer "martyrdom" for the GOSPEL1.Cor.13: 3

All four great gifts and powers are worthless, without LOVE. For they will be like the four comfortable and posh car seats in a car that does not have an engine, gas and wheels.

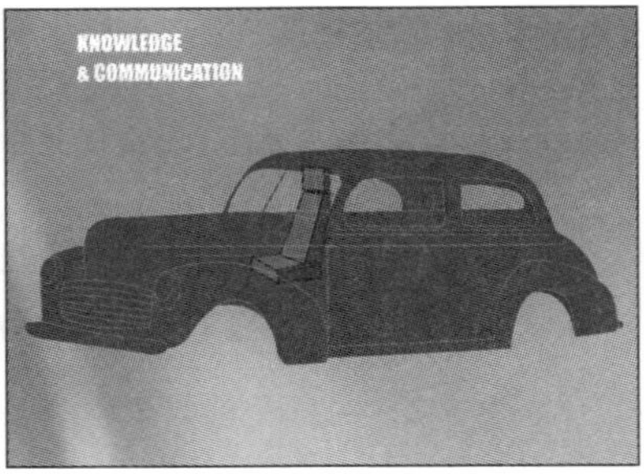

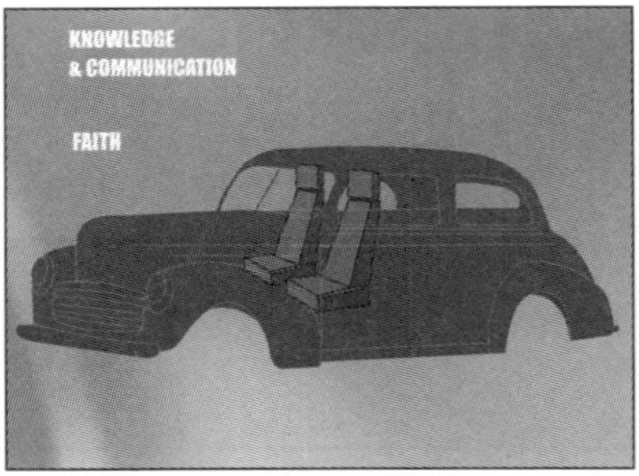

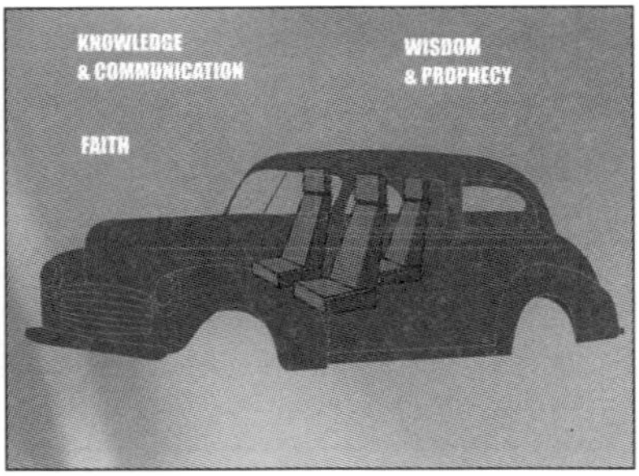

Four elegant comfortable chairs are placed within the frame work of the car.

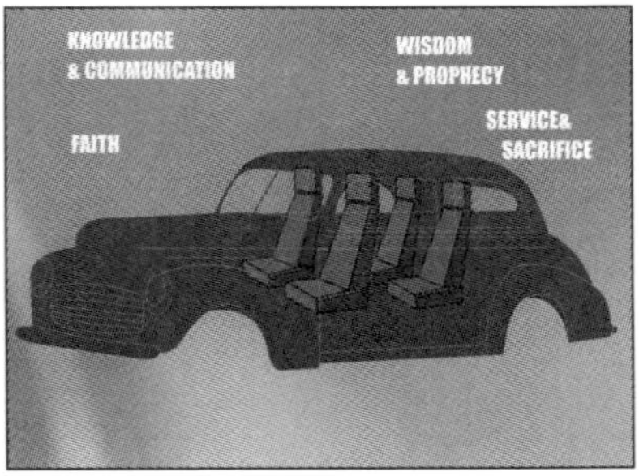

To re-emphasize, we all are on the highway to heaven or hell. We are like the car with four comfortable reclining chairs, each one representing the greatest achievement a human can reach. But the vehicle cannot move just because of these four great luxurious chairs.

Gospel is the message of love from heaven. How can you spread the gospel without love within you? You may preach and teach the gospel – for many different reasons – other than for the love of God. Many Christians and church leaders operate from one of these seats.

The seats give you comfort – a sense of being important. But they do not take you anywhere. They are not of any use without getting connected with God, personally. For we cannot move until the engine, gas tank, the chassis and the wheels are attached.

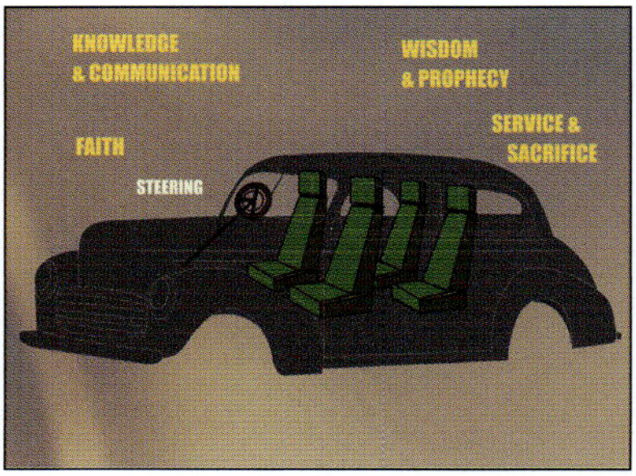

God gives the steering wheel to us

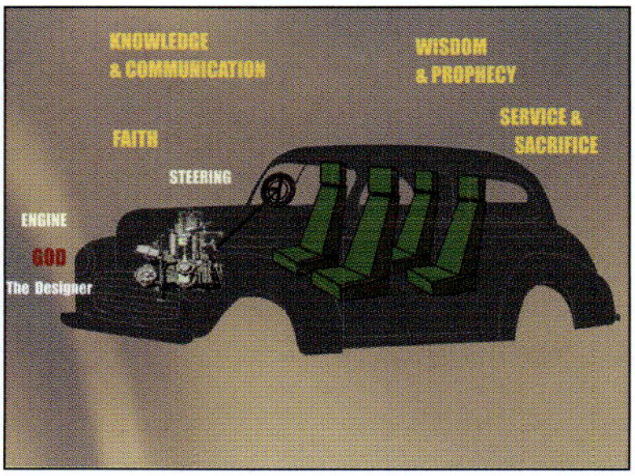

If we seek God, He puts the "Engine" under our bonnets

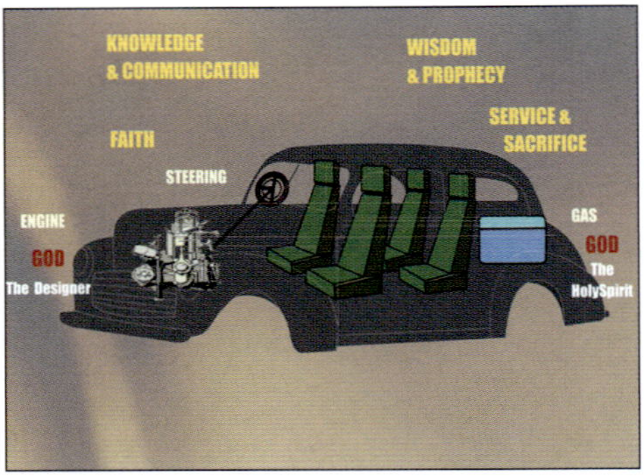

If we welcome the Holy Spirit, that is like the gas tank in the car. However, all the above cannot move any where, yet.

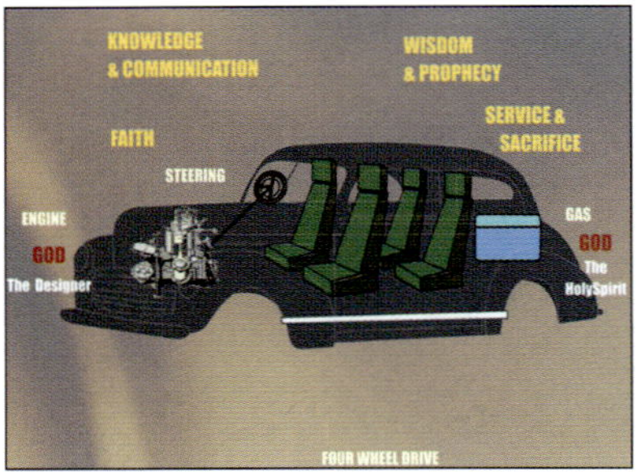

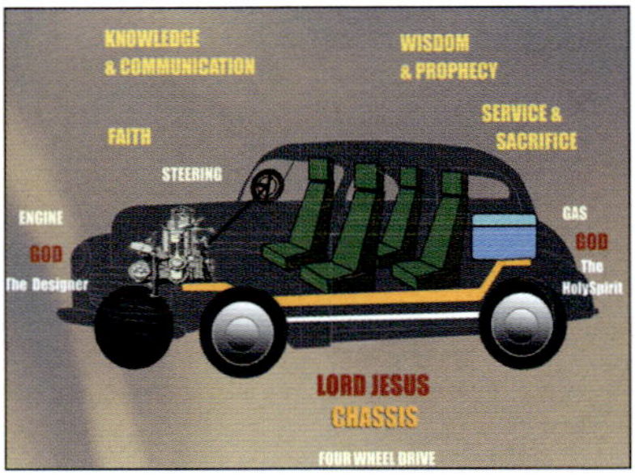

When we receive Jesus into us, He connects the chassis between the engine and the gas. But without the wheels, the car cannot move!

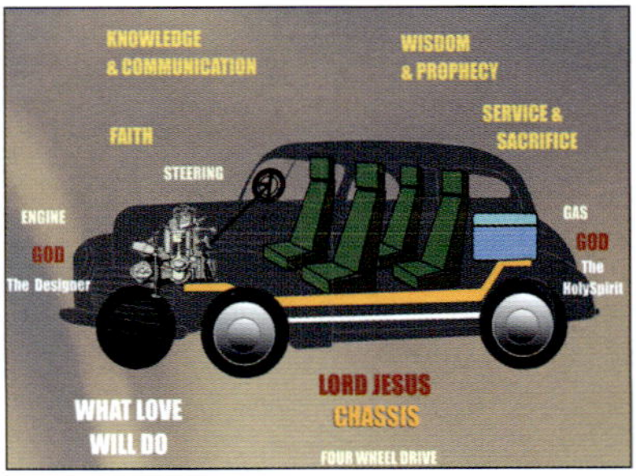

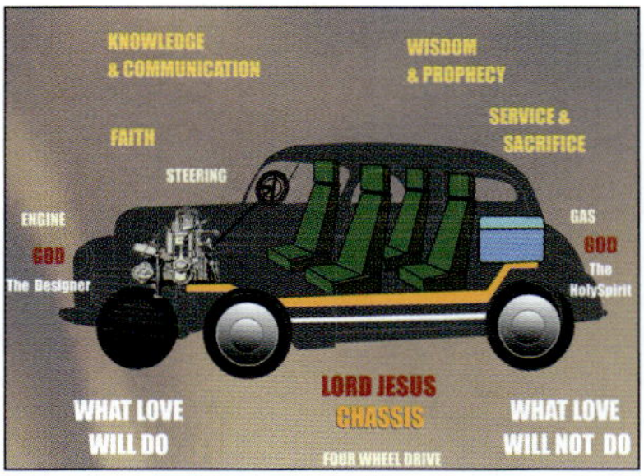

The Wheels are love.

The License to drive are Faith and Hope

THE FRONT WHEELS

What love will do

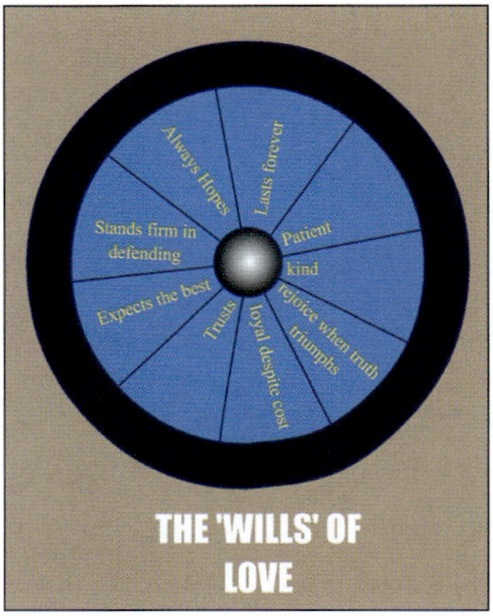

Love will be kind under all circumstances.
Love will be patient even under trying conditions.
Love will rejoice in truth and when truth prevails.
Love remains loyal despite the cost, and under all circumstances.
Love trusts without doubting the motives or outward expressions.
Love wants and expects the best for the loved one to be and do the best.
Love is strong in defending the loved one against any and all odds.
Love always hopes the best for the loved one.
Love has no end, for it is eternal.
Even faith and hope will come to an end in Heaven, but not love.
Wheels carry out our will and willingness.

The wheels need to be always and properly connected to the hub. The hub is connected with the Chassis, Jesus Christ. This is a front wheel drive, for ease and moneuverability.

Brakes are not on front wheels.

There are two sets of wheels in the front and two in the back [right and left]- one side for God, and the other side for "others"- our neighbors, whether they are good or bad, whether they are Christians or Non-Christians.

BACK WHEELS:

WHAT LOVE WILL NOT DO

The 11 "is or will-not" 'Spokes' in the back wheel.

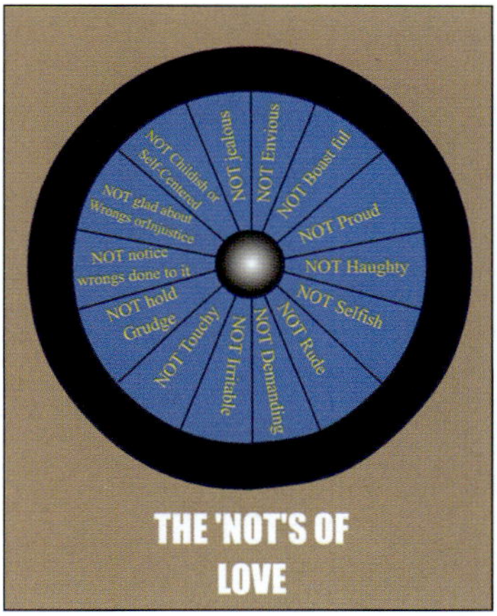

Love is Not touchy
Love does Not hold grudges
Love is Not jealous
Love is Not envious
Love is Not boastful
Love is Not proud
Love is Not haughty
Love is Not selfish
Love is Not rude
Love does Not demand its way
Love is Not irritable

Love will Not notice any wrongs done to it. Love will Not be glad about wrongs or injustice. Love will Not be childish, or, be self centered.

The Spokes of the wheels have spoken!

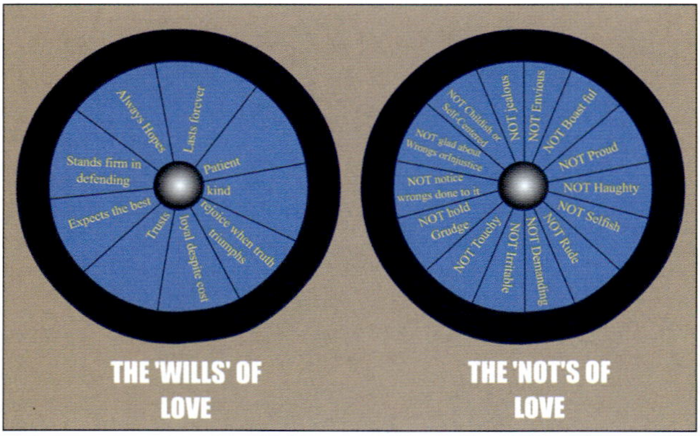

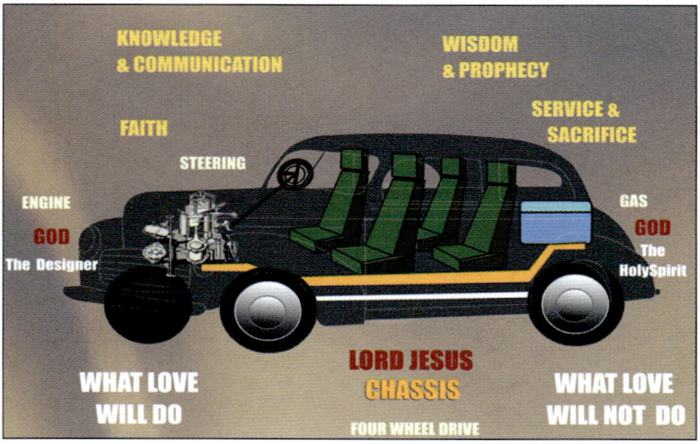

We may step on the gas pedal for acceleration, because of our Zeal but we need to step on the breaks too – in order to maintain Moderation. But, this can happen only if the vehicle is moving!

Brakes are on Back Wheels.

Love can switch to four wheel drive under hard conditions– to make it safe upon snow, ice, hills or rough terrain.

Chapter 16

The Quintessence of LOVE
(1Cor. 13 chapter, 1-8, 13)

"If I could speak in any language in heaven or on earth but didn't love others, I would only be making meaningless noise like a loud gong or a clanging cymbal. [2] If I had the gift of prophecy, and if I knew all the mysteries of the future and knew everything about everything, but didn't love others, what good would I be? And if I had the gift of faith so that I could speak to a mountain and make it move, without love I would be no good to anybody. [3] If I gave everything I have to the poor and even sacrificed my body, I could boast about it; but if I didn't love others, I would be of no value whatsoever.

[4] "Love is patient and kind. Love is not jealous or boastful or proud [5] or rude. Love does not demand its own way. Love is not irritable, and it keeps no record of when it has been wronged. [6] It is never glad about injustice but rejoices whenever the truth wins out. [7] Love never gives up, never loses faith, is always hopeful, and endures through every circumstance.

[8] "Love will last forever, but prophecy and speaking in unknown languages and special knowledge will all disappear [13] There are three things that will endure—faith, hope, and love—and the greatest of these is love."

We need to personalize this gift. To get the gift in the best operating mode, We [you and I] must hand over the 'self' to our Maker and our Master and let Him enable us.

SIGNS AND FEATURES OF LOVE: He will give us this love if we ask Him

Love is very patient – Are you patient? Am I?
I Cor.13: 4

Love is kind - Are you? Am I? I Cor.13:4

Love is never jealous – Are you? am I ? I Cor.13: 4

Love is not envious – Are you? am I
(from time to time)? I Cor.13: 4

Love is never boastful – Do you / I boast
or brag? I Cor.13: 4

Love is never proud – Do you /
I have pride? – Pride about what? I Cor.13: 4

Love is never haughty – what about you/me? I Cor.13:5

Love is never selfish –Am I selfish? Or do I rejoice in other's blessings? I Cor.13: 5

Love is never rude – How often do you/I act rudely? I Cor.13: 5

Love does not demand its own way – what about my idea and advice? I Cor.13:5

Love is not irritable – Am I? How often do I scratch, or scorch? I Cor.13: 5

Love is not touchy – How 'sensitive' am I? I Cor.13: 5

Love does not hold grudges – Do grudges (don't) budge from me? I Cor.13: 5

Love does not even know or notice when others do it harm - How easily am I provoked or get irritated or become sullen? I Cor.13: 5

Love is not happy over injustice, when it is done to others! I Cor.13:6

Love rejoices in truth coming through – How often do I conceal truth? I Cor.13: 6

Love is loyal no matter what it may cost. I Cor.13:7

Love does not give up but defends the loved one always I Cor.13:7

Love lasts for ever, even when all
things pass away I Cor. 13: 8

Love is even greater than Faith and Hope I Cor.13:13

For, Faith and Hope are for earth life.
Love is for life on Earth and Heaven.
Jesus said that He is the Way, the Truth,
and the Life.
The Bible says the 'Truth' will set 'one' free.
When we willingly and voluntarily submit our desire
for freedom,
God will free us from the prison called "self".
When we willingly die to our self, and let Him live
freely in and through us,
We will live as Jesus lived, and love as Jesus loves.

Prayer

Dear God,

I am like a small pebble of hard rock in the bottom of a deep ocean of Your immense love.

I am surrounded and pressed down on all sides by your love. But deep within me, I am dry and devoid of even the moisture of love. Please let me become porous, allowing Your love to flow through me, so as to love You and others around me. May Your life giving water flow out of me in such a way that the water is available without limit to others.

Help me so that I will become small and invisible,
while Christ becomes visible to others.
I ask this in the name of the one who loves you and me.

Amen.

Acknowledgements:

Flash Illustrations— Dr. Suresh Kumar. B.V. Sc.
Front and back cover design—Mr. Vinay Manda B.Com.

Bible References— obtained with the help
of 'Wordsearch7' software.

Computer graphics, formatting, and proof reading help —

Mr. David Phani
Mr. Leslie Samuel
Mr. Vinay Manda

Proof-reading—Miss Beulah Johnson

Dr. Andrew Johnson
Dr. Rajkumar Johnson
Mr. Manicka Chella

References :

1. Topical guide to the Bible. N.I.V. version
Edited by Walter A. Elwell and Douglas Buckwalter
Baker Books
Grand Rapids. Michigan 49516

2. Where to find it in the Bible.
The ultimate A to Z resource
By Ken Anderson
Thomas Nelson Publishers
Nashville 1996

3. WORDsearch7
NavPress
iExalt Electronic publishing

The following is the list of other books the author has written over the years:.

Escape From A Deserter's Death Penalty

An academic physician's candid personal testimony and His documentation of the various emotional sicknesses, which are dangerous to our lives and health; how to be prepared to deal with them. Because his own death sentence was waived, he has waived the charges for the book. It is therefore yours free, for the asking. Visit our website to get more details.

Radiology for the Soul

202 nuggets in the pathway of our lives are presented in rhymes. Some are sharp stones and need to be avoided, some are like stable rocks in marshy areas of path to help us use as stepping stones. These are like the help provided for us by the traffic lights. We need to understand traffic rules and recognize the signs to reach our destination.

ISBN 0-9769249-3-5 $4.95

Crumbs under the Royal Table

A daily devotional of about 3 minutes a day, for the people living in this frantic, hurried, time hungry, environment. This book will meet the need of the reader's hunger and thirst for life. Crumbs- they are not stale, but fresh and do not lack in nourishment.

ISBN 0-9769249-1-9 $9.95

A Tamil translation of this daily devotional is available in Chennai, South India.

The Lord's Prayer

Acknowledges the role of The Father, Son, and the Holy Spirit in the Lord's Prayer. It takes us into receiving the kinship with God, the responsibilities of the citizenship, the acknowledgement of the kingship of God, accepting the Lordship of the Son, restoring the relationship with our neighbors, submission to the discipleship through the Holy Spirit, our role in God's battle against evil, and our worship of the Triune God.

ISBN 1-59581-103-6 $6.75

War of our cultures is feeding the Vultures

A Physician's candid look at the causes for our moral diseases in the modern culture. Diseases flourish when there is lack of hygiene and these in turn result in an epidemic and kill millions around the globe. Lack of mental hygiene and deliberate toxic dumping on the public will destroy the nations around the globe. The key for the clean up is presented.

ISBN 1-594676-81-X $9.99

Deadly Snake Bite

Thousands die every year because of venomous snake bites on the land and in the water. Antivenin is the only possible help for those bitten. All humans have been bitten by the venomous serpent and the venom of sin will kill us, unless we get the antivenin administered to us in time. The Old Testament is the diagnostic component, pointing to 'sin' as the venom killing us. The New Testament is the treatment part offering to us the antivenin for sin, prepared by God through His own blood.

ISBN 0-9769249-0-0 $7.95

CPR from Above

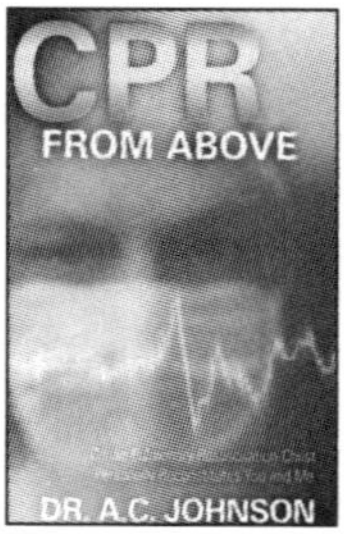

CPR has now become a public priority to let every one learn how to help a person whose heart has stopped due to various causes. For all are becoming aware that if there is no oxygen (air supply) to the brain for three minutes, the brain may be damaged severely and if there is no oxygen to the brain for five minutes, the brain will die. As the heart pumps the blood containing oxygen in its red cells to the brain, the heart has to be manually pumped - and as oxygen has to be obtained from air, air has to be blown into the lungs while the heart is being mechanically pumped.

Many have come back to life, after this procedure. These 5 minutes are crucial. If we give God even 5 minutes a day – He will revive and rejuvenate our hearts, lungs, and minds- not only for this world, but also for the next.

ISBN 1-59781-125-4 $17.00

Anger is Murder in the mind.

This book is meant to help young people to overcome and deal with their anger in a positive way. It is richly illustrated by drawings of young people of different age groups. It addresses the common causes for anger, and the natural outcome of anger when it is not properly dealt with. In the present global age, not only the adults, but even children in kindergarten are becoming victims of anger and violence. The educated adults do not know how to deal with it, as they themselves are victims of anger. This book offers the one and only well tested way to control anger. The material in this book is not only for the young people, but for adults as well.

ISBN 0-9769249-2-7

Anger the deadly time-bomb in our hearts.

Anger is like a tree with its numerous 'bad roots'. The roots feed, support, and hold the trunk and the tree

and its fruits above the ground for people to see. The anger tree and its bad fruits are hazardous to human health. They cause many chronic and deadly diseases like heart attacks, paralyzing strokes, and breakdown of our immune system. The commonly used modern therapeutic systems have not been able to get any control on anger. A new look on a time honored, well documented treatment offered in a 2000 year old unfaultable New Testament is presented as the only successful method of getting a control on anger. Mr. Gandhi and Rev. Martin Luther King adopted the principles in the New Testament, and were able to help mankind. A work book on anger control is also incorporated, combining medical knowledge and principles that are to be applied.

Work Book for Stress, Tension, Anxiety, Fear, Depressions, and Anger.

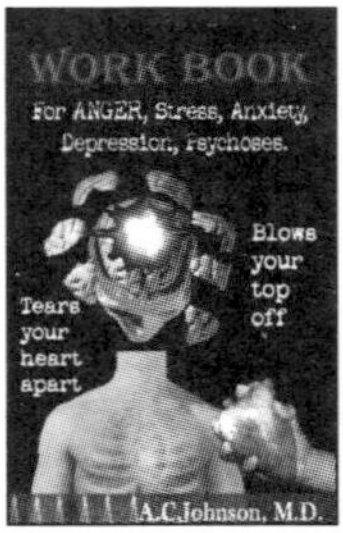

The book offers solution not only for anger, but also for other negative emotions like fears, anxiety, worry, tensions and stresses of different types. Satan the serpent has bitten mankind and has caused many sicknesses of the body and mind. The venom has killed us spiritually. Our mind is part of our soul which Satan is trying to destroy. Jesus became human to give His blood as the only effective antidote for the serpent bite. The body has two major mechanisms to deal with all kinds of venom such as stress, anger, anxieties, depressions and tensions, operating through the autonomic nervous system and the endocrine system. One of them activates and the other calms us down to keep the balance or equilibrium. If not, depressions, psychotic changes and personality changes occur. The only proven antidotes are presented for us to peruse and to use.

Triangle illustrations as work Tool for Anger Control

A visual presentation of various causes for anger that makes us get upset are shown. Biblical methods, and illustrations are offered to enable God to 'reset' us, and to make us grow spiritually. The format will also help teachers to educate and enable people of all ages to be benefited. The truth is that God is our head and we, all the people of different nations, color, caste, creed, language and religion are like different parts of one body. We need to be connected with God as He is our head and with one another as members of the body. The dangers of our disconnection to God and others are brought to the attention of the reader.

Upcoming Books

1. God save our homes.
2. Holistic view of body, Soul and Spirit.
3. High way traffic signs for Heaven or Hell.
4. The Biblical syndromes for you.
5. The rainbow –The Electro magnetic spectrum.
6. Waltz through the Bible.
7. Why are we to be salt and light?